Mr & Mrs Stephen Clemens
2912 E 24th St
Minneapolis MN 55406-1322

Jesus' Radical Message

Jesus' Radical Message

Subversive Sermons for Today's Seekers

Z HOLLER

WIPF & STOCK · Eugene, Oregon

JESUS' RADICAL MESSAGE
Subversive Sermons for Today's Seekers

Wipf & Stock
An Imprint of Wipf and Stock Publishers
199 W. 8th Ave., Suite 3
Eugene, OR 97401
www.wipfandstock.com

ISBN 13: 978-1-60899-267-6

Manufactured in the U.S.A.

For Charlene, the love of my life:
incomparable wife, mother, and grandmother.
So patient with her husband,
who for a third of a century failed to finish
his weekly sermon preparation
before the wee hours of Sunday morning.
Now, at last, we can enjoy our Saturday evenings together.
Thanks be to God!

Contents

Foreword

As an African American child growing up in Halifax County in eastern North Carolina in the 1940s and '50s, I was painfully aware of the racial divide, which was characterized by the routine devaluing and the occasional brutalizing of people of color. The descendants of the owners of my slave ancestors on my mother's side lived two miles down a country road from where I grew up with four brothers and four sisters. My parents sometimes bought groceries at the store operated by that same family that had once owned our family.

Although folk "got along" for the most part, the customs and behaviors in our community taught us to "know our place." Consequently, I grew up with a keen and bitter awareness of the injustices rooted in race. As a teenager, I was beaten up in Charlotte for trying to sit on the front seat of a bus. Frightened and humiliated, I was ultimately forced to go to the back. Through that experience and others like it, I slowly reached a clear resolve that my life would be dedicated to relieving the suffering of others, especially those of my own race.

My relationship with Z Holler began about twenty years ago. We met at a gathering of religious leaders in Greensboro, North Carolina, where we both live. A stray bullet had killed a young African American girl in our city. In response to the senseless loss of a child's life in a crime-ridden, drug-infested public housing project, black and white religious leaders had gathered to bemoan this tragic incident.

I imagine that similar meetings were taking place across the South about such heart-wrenching occurrences. Yet it seemed to me that there was very little understanding among those in attendance about how this event was linked to an entire history of which we were all a part. How it connected to the preaching that was being done every Sunday in both black and white churches seemed even less apparent.

What stood out for me in that meeting was a lean, somewhat soft-spoken white Presbyterian minister named Zeb Holler (His friends call him Z). He seemed genuinely touched, and he wanted to learn more. I use the word *genuinely* because in so many of these gatherings, there is a form of "tipping one's hat" to a problem but an unwillingness to engage issues at both their spiritual and historical roots.

While life had equipped Z and me with different perspectives and different understandings of history and society, I sensed in Z a humility that allowed him to hear deeply the pain and concerns of others. It was the kind of hearing that made him available to grow in his understanding. Coupled with courage, it enabled him to engage what God was revealing to him.

Early in our relationship, I recall riding with Z from a meeting at the Church of the Savior in Washington, D.C., which was founded by Gordon and Mary Cosby. Greensboro was among the first communities to establish a servant leadership school under the tutelage of the Church of the Savior. On the way home from that trip, I learned some things about Z that significantly increased my respect for him.

About twelve years earlier, in November 1979, I was the lead organizer of an anti-Klan and pro-labor march and conference. The legally planned march never took place. An armed caravan of Ku Klux Klan and American Nazi Party members attacked the marchers at the assembly point. Five people were killed, ten others were wounded, including myself, and the public housing community where the march was to begin was terrorized. The entire city of Greensboro was thrown into shock.

The Greensboro Massacre, as it came to be known, was then and remains today one of the most fear-laden experiences in the history of our city. In 2002, twenty-three years after the event, the Greensboro Truth and Community Reconciliation Project was established to bring people together to talk about that terrible day and its enduring impact. Based on international models, it was the first of its kind in the United States. The Truth Commission's 529-page report, growing out of nearly two years of intense work, is helping to lead Greensboro out of the long night of fear, bitterness, and division.

During our drive back from Washington, Z and I discussed that difficult and wrenching time in the history of our city. He told me that the owner of the funeral home that had received four of the five bodies of those killed was fearful of taking the bodies to the burial site. The whole city was under curfew, and a state of martial law had been declared. The National Guard encircled the city and accompanied the funeral procession with bayonets drawn. In this tense atmosphere, Z volunteered to ride in the lead hearse to the burial site to help calm the fears of the funeral home owner.

Z Holler is my friend. He has taught me much. I believe we have been a source of mutual inspiration and growth for each other. In this book of sermons, we find an encapsulation of the journey and life strivings of a humble, yet powerful, Southern white Presbyterian preacher. Z has consistently allowed himself to be vulnerable as he has interacted throughout his ministry with a variety of persons whose backgrounds are very different from his own. His sermons reflect that.

These sermons were not prepared for a book. They were prepared and preached as relevant gospel messages that sought to speak to the changing needs of people over a span of more than fifty years. The sermons engage the raw edges of life, including the many faces of our inhumanity toward one another, not the least of which is racism.

Some people listen to sermons because they feel obligated to listen. They attend church out of habit. Often they wish they were elsewhere, yet feel obligated to be present, so they endure the sermon. Others listen to sermons because the content is entertaining and tends to confirm the hearers where they are.

Then there are listeners who listen because they are drawn by the message of love, hope, and new possibilities—a message that engages them at their core, connects them to all of humanity, and challenges them to "take up their cross" and make the world a better place, while becoming better persons themselves. Z is very much a preacher who speaks to the third type of listener. His sermons are convicting, humbling, and hopeful.

I serve as pastor of Faith Community Church in Greensboro. It is a small, predominately African American church that is frequented by many homeless people, former addicts and prisoners, and others existing on the margins of life. Occasionally Z preaches at Faith Community Church. Although he has a very different style of preaching from mine, his messages have a penetrating power that speaks to the inner core of the hearers.

Hearers often attest to the lessons learned from Z's sermons for weeks afterward—a true testimony to the power of his preaching. So the sermons that you will read in this book are not just Sunday talk. As demonstrated by Z's presence in that funeral march, they reflect a deep faith in the gracious care of a generous God.

Z Holler is my brother. As I matured, I learned that injustices are not only reflected in racial behaviors but also in class, gender, ethnicity, and many other arbitrary categories that marginalize or divide people and affect the way they value others different from themselves. Our problem is what Z calls the human condition, the result of being born in sin and reared in iniquity.

Though our journeys have been very different, Z and I have worked shoulder to shoulder over the last many years through some good times and some very difficult ones. I have often endured blistering public criticism, but Z has never wavered in loyalty to me and to our friendship. Together with others we formed the Beloved Community Center. Drawing on the moral, religious, and faith heritage that has spawned a continuous tradition of social reform in this nation, we have sought to actualize the beloved community in Greensboro and beyond.

If you sit with Z's sermons, you will sense in him an understanding of providence and a gift of real humility, with a pinch of humor. His reflections are all anchored in a clear understanding of the deteriorating global conditions growing out of our corporate culture. Z's sermons can provide renewing encounters for the minds and spirits that yet hold out the possibility and hope for a transformed society in which the dignity, worth, and enormous unrealized potential of all of God's children can be realized.

Nelson N. Johnson

Acknowledgments

It would be quite impossible to acknowledge all of the teachers, parishioners, and loved ones whose wisdom and example through the years have enriched my life and my understanding of Jesus and his message. My parents and the other adults in our family connection who nurtured me, the teachers in the public schools and the Sunday school of my early years, and later, my college and seminary professors and the patient parishioners of the churches and other ministries in which I have served—all have offered sustaining support and regular reminders of God's astonishing love and care. These have brought joy and blessings to Charlene (my wife of fifty-six years), to me, and to our family amid the joys and trials of our life together in this tumultuous age.

I give thanks to God as I gladly acknowledge these loved ones and friends and the institutions they represent for their faithful witness, candid criticisms, and guidance. These have deepened my understanding and my faith in God, while Jesus has continued to call me—to call all of us who claim him—to confront the truth about our death-dealing ways and the liberating, life-giving possibilities of the world of justice and beloved community for which he gave himself and which he calls us to serve in his spirit.

Finally, I would be remiss if I failed to acknowledge the editorial wisdom, amazing patience, and encouragement of my editor and friend, Joyce Hollyday. Without Joyce's gracious, persistent, professional advice and help, this book would not have been published.

Introduction

L ET'S BE HONEST ABOUT our situation. Can we continue in the direction our world is headed at present without bringing disaster upon ourselves and upon the other species with whom we share this planet? Our egocentric competitiveness is out of control. Think of the children you know, dressed in their athletic gear or their dancing costumes, struggling to outdo one another and achieve celebrity status. Or observe the parents on the sidelines cheering the kids on, blasting the coaches' or the officials' decisions when those decisions go against their sons and daughters. Or think of the owners and managers of businesses large and small, struggling by all means, fair means if possible, foul means if necessary, to maintain their market share.

And what if things don't go our kid's way or our corporation's way? What if our governmental bodies' leaders are in disarray, an embarrassment for us locally and a threat to our reputation and position of power among the nations? Who or what is to blame? Sorry parents? Irresponsible, undisciplined children? A bad marriage? Greedy, incompetent managers? Untrustworthy leaders? Even untrustworthy church leaders? Or all of the above? Including me?

Well, yes. After all, aren't all of us sinners living in a sinful world? Pogo, the comic strip character, put it this way: "We have met the enemy and they is us." And who can deny it? For our world to get better, we must change—*all* of us.

So here is the point of the book you have in your hands: God's prescription for what ails us is available to us all in the astonishingly gracious life and challenging message of Jesus of Nazareth. As I see it, God has given both direction and power for the radical change we need in the gift of Jesus' life and teachings. Nothing less than Jesus' radical challenge to the sinful, self-destructive society of his day and our day can shake us loose from our fearful acceptance of "the way things are."

If, out of fear, we are content to continue in our present mode, we may self-destruct and take large numbers of the Earth's other inhabitants with us. But what if, under the gracious influence of Jesus, we were to turn from our self-destructive ways and embrace the way of love and service that he embodied? What then? A changed life? A changed world?

God only knows. But I have great hope. Jesus embodied no less than God's will of healing for us all. This is the message that we desperately need to hear, understand, and heed today, if we are to be messengers of hope and healing for this world.

Jesus' radical, world-changing deeds and words are the subject of the collection that follows. They are words that point to the heart of what I have learned with fellow sinners as we have sought to know and serve with the most gracious, courageous friend and Servant of us all.

Most of the items in this volume were born as sermons. But they are not what one might call "typical" sermons, if there is such a thing. Let me explain. A hearer of one of my earliest sermons smiled as he left the church, wrung my hand, then looked at me quizzically and declared, "You aren't a preacher, you're a teacher."

His unexpected comment struck me at first as a put-down. But upon further consideration, I concluded that it was an honest response to a message intended to stimulate study, discussion, and action, rather than to proclaim authoritative answers to questions concerning the church's life and mission. My sermon had lacked the familiar rhetoric, style, and content that he expected of a preacher. This brother's blunt comment has stayed with me over the years and helped me to preach and teach not as a "religious authority" but as a fellow seeker and a servant of other seekers of God.

If these are not "typical" sermons, how might one describe them? They are intended to be "disturbing sermons." *Disturbing sermons??* Let's face it: most sermons are not terribly disturbing.

Yet Jesus' sermons are *very* disturbing. They shake us to the roots of our being and challenge us to new possibilities. Take his Sermon on the Mount found in the fifth through seventh chapters of the Gospel of Matthew, for instance. That sermon—or, more accurately, that "radical teaching"—is about as subversive of our modern American values and practices—and of most of our world's values and practices—as anything I can imagine. If you read those chapters of Matthew for yourself, I believe you will see what I mean.

The challenging words recorded there are the sort that got Jesus into big trouble. His message was not like the Sunday morning preaching in most churches of my experience. Most sermons that I have heard and preached over a lifetime are nothing near as unsettling as Jesus' Sermon on the Mount. Usually they have been aimed at reinforcing the religious feelings and commitments of church members and urging them to greater loyalty to their church's beliefs and programs.

Such preaching can be personally and institutionally helpful, I admit. But that sort of traditional preaching, along with the "mainline" churches in which it has been most prevalent over the years, has lost its appeal to growing numbers of our neighbors who are caught up willy-nilly in the dangers and confusion of our fragmented modern world. Like me, they need challenging, life-changing help of the sort that Jesus offers. That's the kind of help I'm trying to reflect in this collection of sermons that you hold in your hands.

Julia Strope, a candid colleague, questioned me after reading one of the pieces in this collection. She wanted to know what audience I had in mind in publishing these sermons: "Preachers over sixty? Preachers under sixty? Seekers?" Good question.

The settings where these messages were first preached or taught were indeed churches, and more often than not, Presbyterian churches. I certainly had those church folk in mind as my hearers when I preached in those settings. But since my official "retirement" in 1993, the audience has expanded.

In recent years, I have been called on to preach and teach in a variety of churches and other settings. Consequently, I've spoken to hearers of all ages and various races: devout and conventional Christians, disillusioned former believers, agnostics and atheists, as well as a few persons of other faiths. I have assumed that my hearers were in need of the sort of radical help and healing for their lives that drew all sorts of troubled folk to Jesus two thousand years ago.

That's why I'm focusing this book on Jesus' message as I have learned and am still learning to understand it. His first-century hearers and followers were in a "heap of trouble" then, and so are we today. So these days I am trying to help varied groups of brothers and sisters to listen to the message of Jesus' life as God gives us understanding of it, and then do what Jesus leads us to do as we spread that good news to others whom we touch, whoever and wherever they may be.

In answer to Julia's question, the audience I have in mind is "seekers of all sorts." Certainly those who gather for Christian worship or study. But also other seekers who in various settings are willing to give Jesus a respectful hearing, or even engage one another in serious reflection and conversation concerning their hopes and fears and their intended actions in response to Jesus' challenge to the moral and spiritual confusion that plagues our world.

I have been such a seeker for most of my life. And today I have more hope for our suffering world and a more solid foundation for service among all sorts and conditions of folk I meet than I could have imagined a few short years ago. I have a passionate desire to share with the broadest possible circle of fellow seekers what I have gleaned from my experience with neighbors of all sorts, from whom and with whom I have continued to learn as a follower of Jesus.

Though these sermons were first offered in congregational and educational church settings, most of them reached their present form after I started working as a volunteer with three related community ministries: 1) The Beloved Community Center of Greensboro, North Carolina, which was established by a biracial group that is committed to carrying on the spirit of Dr. Martin Luther King, Jr's work for racial and economic justice and reconciliation; 2) Faith Community Church, a small, predominantly African American congregation that shares the vision and many of the staff, as well as the facilities, of the Beloved Community Center; and 3) The Servant Leadership School of Greensboro, modeled on a similar school founded by the Church of the Savior in Washington, D.C., which helps a very diverse group of seekers grow in their "inward journey" of personal transformation and their "outward journey" of life-giving service. (More information on each of these ministries is available in the book's Appendices.) What I have learned from the unusually diverse group of colleagues with whom I am working in these endeavors of faith has deepened my commitment to Jesus' way of embodying God's love— and to Jesus' liberating (and let's admit it, *subversive*) challenge to the "real world" of our global society of today.

My biblical explorations are intended to encourage and empower not only congregations of Jesus' followers, but also any and all who—like the participants in the Beloved Community Center, Faith Community Church, and the Servant Leadership School—are seeking God's healing and transforming purpose for their lives and the world. Amid the destructive social and personal pressures created by our nation's pursuit and exploitation of its position of global dominance, these messages are invitations to modern seekers to turn from our consumer society's death-dealing ways and values (in biblical terms, "to repent") and to trust the good news of God's beloved community ("the kingdom of God"), proclaimed and embodied in Jesus' life and ministry as God's powerful new possibility for all of the unruly human family. The Presbyterian Christian lineage of the messages will sometimes be evident to my readers but never, I trust, in ways that would demean or exclude those belonging to other Christian groups, or other faiths, or those of secular humanist or atheistic persuasion.

About the Interpreter

FRIENDS HAVE ENCOURAGED ME to include some autobiographical material concerning influences that have shaped my life, so that readers may better understand "where this fellow is coming from." I appreciate their suggestion. After all, the Bible is a book of very human testimony to the character and purposes of the Creator of the universe. Its witnesses tell of how God has been revealed through the experience of the communities of which they were a part. The biblical writers speak always out of their experience and that of their community, with its story and traditions. It follows that their testimony can rightly be understood only in the light of the perspectives and experiences—the historical context—out of which they are speaking.

Surely the same is true of witnesses to God's presence and purposes and actions in the events of our time. We who preach and teach today have been shaped by events and influences, and by the values and history of our society and our place within it. For this reason, it is only fair and responsible for me to confess to you, my readers, the sort of life experience that influenced my interpretations of the treasures of the biblical witness.

"August 2, 1928" is the mantra that I'm required to repeat over and over when I go to the doctor's office for the various tests and treatments required to keep one with such a birth date alive and functioning in our fast-moving society. Within a few years (three? four?) of my birth, the following event occurred—as told by my mother and vaguely remembered by me.

We children had been taught in Sunday school one morning that God is everywhere. That got my attention. So I told Digie (everyone called my mother by that nickname) about it as she was preparing Sunday dinner after church. Then I walked into our dining room, came back, and asked, "Digie, is God in *there*?"

"Yes," she said.

Next I went to the living room, some distance from the kitchen, came back and asked, "Is God in there?"

"Yes," said she.

Then I went to my bedroom, returned shortly, and asked again, "Is God in there, too?"

"God is everywhere," my mother assured me.

And I said, "That sounds fishy to me."

Whether or not it happened just so, I can't say, but this is the way I remember my mother telling the story years later. Certainly it is true to my life experience. I have never been able to believe what others urged me to believe when their beliefs made no sense to me.

Digie also told this story from that formative period in my life. One afternoon I rode my tricycle down to the neighbors' house. They were playing bridge on their front porch with some friends. I got off the tricycle, stood and watched them play. They were telling stories and pronouncing them "marvelous" as they laughed and played.

Soon they noticed me standing there, and one of them asked me who I was and where I lived. I told them. And then I commented that *my* mother didn't play bridge and say "marvelous" and things like that. Of course the bridge players gleefully reported this item of self-righteous candor to my embarrassed mother. I'm still struggling to exorcise the demon of self-righteousness that possessed me that day and regularly afflicts me still.

The experience of growing up in Greensboro, North Carolina, was a happy one for me and I believe for the family and friends with whom I shared it. I attended public schools, which were racially, and to a large extent economically, segregated. My classmates were all white and mostly middle class like us, many having college-educated parents who were teachers, merchants, small business owners or employees of larger companies, as my father was. We lived near the center of the city. Greensboro's textile villages were outlying, so the children of white textile workers went to schools in their own neighborhoods. The children of the city's wealthy inhabitants usually attended private schools, or public schools in their more-affluent suburban areas.

With the exception of sporadic enclaves in a few white neighborhoods like ours, African Americans lived in the southeastern part of the city. There, two excellent institutions of higher learning, Bennett College for women and North Carolina A&T (Agricultural and Technical) State

University, provided opportunities for higher education and cultural enrichment for the mostly low-income black residents of that part of town. The public schools in those neighborhoods were a source of pride for their constituencies. The marching bands from the black schools were consistently the most talented, energetic, and entertaining of all the bands in our city's Christmas parades. But, for the most part, social, racial, and economic segregation was the rule in Greensboro. White leaders kept the city under their control, and those like me tended to mind our own business, accepting "the way things are."

Growing up with "my own kind" in such a segregated city, I acquired an unexamined, and largely unconscious, prejudice against African Americans and poor whites. With it came a prejudice also against labor organizing, which was an expanding enterprise among both the black and white workers of our state's large textile industry. The efforts during World War II of John L. Lewis, the tough Welsh organizer of the United Mine Workers, were represented in our media and in conversation with my peers as unpatriotic. My friends and I grew up thinking of such labor organizers and the workers who supported them as dangerous troublemakers. Not until my senior year in high school, when I had an excellent American history teacher (an imposing woman whom we called "Bull" Smith!), were my eyes opened to the critical importance of the labor movement for underpaid and exploited workers.

My family attended the Presbyterian Church of the Covenant, a liberal, openhearted congregation, where I received a lot of love and a sense of the goodness and righteousness of God. I received the same at home. One of my happiest memories is sitting in my father's lap listening to his reading of a book I knew as "Hurlbert's Bible stories." For my parents, the Christian faith mattered not primarily as a set of beliefs to be accepted as the condition of forgiveness by God and assurance of eternal life, but as a life to be lived with honesty, integrity, and compassion.

At table our family often talked of care and concern for others, especially life's excluded "underdogs." Bullying anybody (especially black people), or allowing anyone to be bullied or demeaned, was very wrong in our eyes. Such was the spirit of our family and of our church. But there were no black Christians in our church. The rationale that was often given: "They have their own churches."

We did worship with African Americans on one occasion, the memory of which I cherish. The college choirs of Bennett College (black),

Greensboro College (white), Women's College of the University of North Carolina (white), and a singing group from A&T State University (black) put on a joint Christmas program at the First Presbyterian Church of Greensboro (white). I remember the experience as thrilling musically and amazing socially—the most racially integrated of my childhood. But it was the exception. Jim Crow was the rule.

Our pastor, R. Murphy Williams, was in effect a pastor to the entire community—a much-loved character who visited and prayed with most patients in the local hospitals, whoever they were and whatever their condition (My mother observed that he seemed always to drop by her hospital room when she was on the bed pan!). I would guess that he visited black friends of his when they were hospitalized, but I don't know for sure. I'm not even sure that black people were admitted to any but one of our Greensboro hospitals on a regular basis. That one was theirs.

Rev. Williams regularly visited in many of the businesses and offices downtown, inviting those he encountered there to "Come worship with us at the Church of the Covenant this Sunday!" With a big heart, open to all, he stood at the door and embraced everyone as the members left church events. Known throughout the city as "R. Murphy, " he was a real man of the people, unique in his energetic engagement in community affairs and in his active good will toward all sorts and conditions of people.

One Sunday, when I was about ten or eleven years old, Rev. Williams gave me a hug as I was leaving church. He told me that he had been noticing how attentive I was during worship and suggested that I should think about becoming a minister. I was flabbergasted! But I remembered his words and was seriously considering the ministry a few years later as I entered Davidson College in 1945.

There, however, I met some conservative Bible-quoting "pre-ministerial" classmates whose pious, doctrinaire ways I couldn't swallow (seemed sorta "fishy" to me!). Neither could I stomach the bland "churchiness" of others in the pre-ministerial group. With my self-righteous demons thus revived, I put my thoughts of ministry and my initial identification with "pre-ministerials" on hold.

After graduating from Davidson in 1949, I taught high school English and coached football for a year in Lancaster, South Carolina, and greatly enjoyed it. That summer the Korean War commenced, and with it the prospect of my being drafted. So I enlisted in the U.S. Navy flight program, hoping to become a military hero like those I had seen operating off ships in the newsreels of World War II.

While in flight training in Pensacola, Florida, I began to think again of the ministry, partly because of hearing Charlene Levey, a lovely young high school senior, preach at a Youth Sunday service at the Presbyterian church I attended when I was free from weekend duty. A Davidson classmate who lived in Pensacola and knew Charlene got me a date with her, and we hit it off famously. We married in 1953. In little more than a year later, Charlene gave birth to our eldest daughter, Angie.

After my discharge from the Navy in 1955, we moved to Richmond, Virginia, where I attended Union Theological Seminary. There, Charlene finished her college degree at Richmond Professional Institute and gave birth to our second daughter, Ginger. Charlene's achievement during those three years was greater than mine by far! After graduation, I was ordained as a minister of the Presbyterian Church, U.S.

That fall we moved to Scotland for two years, during which I completed the residency requirement for a PhD at the University of Aberdeen. While there, diligently studying the best scholarly work available on the life and ministry of Jesus, I got hold of a book by Martin Dibelius. In it he had gathered the raw materials of the Gospels, the stories of Jesus' encounters with his contemporaries—his healing of lepers, the disabled and demon-possessed, and other outcasts; his respectful and supportive interactions with women and their children; also his exchanges with his detractors and enemies among the religious establishment. In short, all of the early church's vivid memories of Jesus' very human interactions with his contemporaries.

One evening, while in my ice-cold attic study in Aberdeen, I picked up and read Dibelius' book. I was mesmerized by the profound humanity, courage, and compassion of Jesus that these sparkling "jewels" of the early Christians' memories of him displayed. This encounter with Jesus—not the glorified, larger-than-life Christ of the church's theology and piety, but this astonishing, challenging brother of us all, Jesus of Nazareth—set my heart on fire. From that day to this, I have been his, for better or worse.

In Scotland our family was warmly embraced by our Scottish neighbors and fellow students. As Americans we were something of a curiosity. So I was asked by a Scottish friend to speak one Sunday with her Sunday school class at Queens Cross Church. At one point in the discussion, a member of the class quizzed me about American society: "How do you deal with the fact that in America you actually have two nations, one white and the other black?"

I was startled and embarrassed by the question. "It's not like that!" said I. "Why, some of my best friends are black," etc., etc., etc. Despite my protestations, that was the moment when I began to realize how deeply rooted Southern, white, racist prejudices were in my soul. I vowed to break free, and help others break free, from this racist heritage.

When we returned to the United States in 1960, I was called to serve as pastor of the Young Memorial Associate Reformed Presbyterian Church in Anderson, South Carolina. The civil rights struggle was already well under way. I did my best to address the racial issues of the time in the disturbing light of the gospel, and in keeping with my vow to break free and help free others from the shackles of racism.

The small congregation proved remarkably gracious in responding to my countercultural teaching and preaching efforts, and in offering our family joyful support upon the arrival of our son, Roy Kemp. Charlene and I named Roy for my best friend in Scotland, Bert Kemp, who was Clerk of the Session at Tullynessle and Forbes, the small, warm, and welcoming parish church where I had served as supply preacher. Our son's name is an enduring reminder of the many friendships and the kindness we had known among the Scots.

The congregation at Young Memorial also offered us much love and sympathy when, soon after Roy's birth, my father, who had seemed to me to be in vigorous good health for a man of seventy-five, died very suddenly of a massive heart attack. This was a very painful loss. It left me without any sense of closure with Daddy, who had loved and inspired me and shared freely his faith and guidance through the years.

In keeping with the message that Jesus had brought home to us through my work in Scotland, Charlene and I invited some student "freedom riders" to our home in Anderson. They stopped with us for rest and refreshment on their way back to their homes in the Midwest, after their exciting bus rides for desegregation in the Deep South. The local Ku Klux Klan learned of our hospitality and made menacing phone calls to our home, but, surprisingly, failed to carry through on the threats. The congregation supported us through the resulting crisis, which opened up some honest conversation and struggle in our church and in the denomination, as well as in the city of Anderson.

During our four years in the city, I became an officer of the Anderson Ministerial Association and was instrumental in opening the organization to the pastors of the African American congregations in town. Our act of "clergy desegregation" caused considerable stir in the city and occasioned objections from its media and from folks in the white churches, along with more threats from the Klan.

For biblical light on this situation, I turned to Luke's story of Jesus' encounter with a learned seeker, which evoked his parable of the "Good Samaritan" (Luke 10:25–37). I proceeded to preach two "in your face" sermons based on that passage. They were titled "Race Issue I" and "Race Issue II." These were surprisingly well received in that troubled situation. As time has passed and racism has persisted in our society, that parable has often helped me stay in conversation with followers of Jesus who, like me, are struggling with the deep contradictions that our Southern racist heritage imposes on us as white Christians.

A lasting legacy of the years in Anderson was the establishment there of a school of theology for laypersons. I served as a board member and teacher in this ecumenical venture, which continued for many years, offering lay leaders opportunities for serious study of the Christian heritage and its significance for modern life. That experience proved to be helpful preparation for my teaching and leadership with the Servant Leadership School of Greensboro during the years since my retirement.

After four years in Anderson, we returned to Richmond, Virginia, with the hope that I could at long last finish my doctoral dissertation. I served as a supply pastor in Presbyterian churches in the Norfolk area, worked on my dissertation in the Union Seminary Library, and served as an assistant to Professor of Theology John Leith. Charlene furthered her preparation to be a teacher of young children by attending night classes at the Richmond Professional Institute. Soon after our move to Richmond, our daughter Elizabeth was born—a feisty "youngest of the brood," who with her older siblings kept things lively around our house.

At the end of two years in Richmond, I was called to serve as an educator on the pastoral staff of Central Presbyterian Church in the heart of Atlanta, Georgia. There I finally put the finishing touches on my dissertation and received my hard-earned PhD from the University of Aberdeen.

During our first year at Central, the greater part of my work was devoted to developing an experimental church school curriculum, which made use of the vocational and special interests of a number of gifted laypersons in the church and in the Atlanta area. At a meeting in Atlanta's Quaker House, I was introduced to the Black Power movement, as described and embodied enthusiastically by Julius Lester, one of its eloquent spokespersons. Listening to Brother Lester that night was both sobering and enlightening to us liberal whites. He helped me to see how patronizing we had often been in our support of the civil rights struggle.

This was exceptionally good preparation for the next phase of my work in Atlanta, which was focused on renewing relationships within and beyond the congregation, which had become strained during the racial turmoil of the 1960s. This involved, among other efforts, strengthening Central church's relationship with Dr. Martin Luther King, Jr's congregation a few blocks down the street.

In the spring of 1968, Dr. King was assassinated. When some of us at Central went to offer our condolences to the King family and his congregation, we learned that they were going to need much help welcoming and seeing to the needs of the crowds of visitors, many of them very poor, who were coming to Dr. King's funeral. We offered to open up our gym as sleeping accommodation for a couple hundred people.

During the hours of waiting for the first visitors to arrive, the situation was trying, and the volunteers became tense. The State Capitol building directly across the street was closed for the day, and cars full of nervous, heavily armed state troopers lurked behind the bushes and in its driveways. Radio and TV reports of violence elsewhere, and of some fires and vandalism in the Atlanta area, had most of the populace frightened. City Hall, less than a block away, was draped in black crepe, as was the church. During the long hours between sundown on the evening before the funeral and breakfast on the day of the service, the only signs of life in our particular sector of the central city were the traffic in and out of our church and the men in the parked police cars.

On the day of the funeral, we opened our new, previously unused dining room to the crowds of grieving visitors. With generous help from a nearby U.S. Army facility and the local Playboy Club (!), and with volunteers from Agnes Scott College for women and elsewhere, we were able to feed more than five thousand visitors in the course of the day. As black mourners sat at table and white volunteers served, and people from all over the United States and a number of foreign countries ate together, many experienced and expressed a sense of wonder and well-being.

Other people, especially those of our neighbors who had remained in their homes through fear or prudence, expressed their belief that this hospitality was a dangerous mistake that we were lucky to get away with unscathed. Even some of those who participated remained frightened about the wisdom of the church's efforts and worried about what it might mean for us in the future.

But for me—and I believe for many others—it was "God with us" in a moment of (sometimes boisterous) "holy communion." It was surely an encouraging, life-giving moment of Beloved Community: a sort of modern reenactment of Jesus' miracle of the loaves and fishes. For there was plenty of food for all through the sharing, and there was hope shining bright amid all the sorrow and grief.

From time to time during those hours, one's eyes would meet the eyes of a stranger and encounter there an unexpected warmth, an unspoken acknowledgment of the mystery and goodness of it all—a small glimpse of the miracle of reconciliation. After this shared sacrament, we all went out and watched the funeral procession as it passed the church, joining in from time to time with the multitudes who wept and sang "We Shall Overcome" and other hymns of faith and anthems of the civil rights struggle.

A few months later, I accepted a call to serve as the Presbyterian campus minister at North Carolina State University in Raleigh. This new assignment was like being pastor of a congregation of twenty thousand from every kind of religious and ethnic background. The university was my parish, but because many of the students had never heard of a "campus minister" and cared very little for the Christian church and its ministry, it was a bit like being a missionary in a strange land.

The campus was in considerable turmoil over the Vietnam War and the drugs that were arriving regularly from Fort Bragg nearby, usually by way of troubled and addicted veterans returning from their tours of duty in Nam. To add to the resultant confusion, the sexual revolution of that period was well under way and was producing many unwanted pregnancies and a growing traffic in dangerous, illegal abortions. Soon after my arrival, we campus ministers developed a cooperative campus ministry in order to meet these challenges, offering "servant leadership" through draft and drug and abortion counseling to desperate students and pursuing whatever avenues were available to us for maintaining communication with the centers of student life, the university's leaders, local churches, and the larger Raleigh community.

Such was the work that occupied most of my waking moments in Raleigh. Charlene pressed on as a marvelously understanding, longsuffering, overworked wife and mother, who continued developing her skills as a creative teacher of young children—all in the midst of the cultural revolution that was in process in Raleigh during the period when we were living there.

At the end of my years at N.C. State, the Presbytery of which I was a member called me to serve on its staff as a "pastor to pastors" and to congregations that were being torn apart by the tensions of the time. This work required a great deal of travel and struggle with our Presbyterian congregations in order to keep our Presbyterian system and its ecclesiastical interests and structures from devouring the humanity of its members and pastors, as well as its sense of mission. I found the demands of this sort of institutional maintenance to be work for which I was ill prepared and ill suited. So I was greatly relieved after a couple of years when I was unexpectedly called to be pastor of the Fort Hill Presbyterian Church in Clemson, South Carolina, alongside Clemson University.

In Clemson, we were able to put into practice much of what I had learned amid the confusion of the N.C. State campus and through my community and Presbytery service in Raleigh. Happily, our work and our life among the supportive folk of Clemson and the Fort Hill congregation turned out to be a time of rest and rehabilitation for the family. Charlene was able to complete a graduate degree at the university while she further sharpened her teaching skills. All the while, we and our children matured as a family and the Fort Hill church grew and prospered.

In July of 1979, we moved back to Greensboro, where I was called to serve as pastor of the Church of the Covenant in which I was reared. One morning a few weeks after our arrival, I found posters pasted on the wooden screen that the church used for showing movies to neighborhood kids. These posters advertised a "Death to the Klan" labor organizing rally for November 3. I removed the inflammatory posters from our "movie screen" and thought little of it until November 3, the fateful day of the rally.

Local mill owners had been using the Ku Klux Klan to frustrate the organizing of a racially integrated textile union. The rally organizers, who were members at that time of the Communist Workers Party, had envisioned a march through adjoining low-income neighborhoods, mostly

African American, to be followed by an educational event at a nearby African American church. It was planned in terms that were approved by city officials who, after considerable waffling and delay, had finally issued the necessary parade permit for it. Accordingly, the event was to be carried out under the protection of the Greensboro Police Department.

Just before the starting time for the march, a caravan of vehicles loaded with members of the Klan and the American Nazi Party arrived on the scene at the starting point. The tactical squad of the Greensboro Police, which was responsible for the protection of the marchers, had been sent to lunch, in spite of their leader's knowledge that the heavily armed Klan-Nazi caravan was approaching the location where the marchers were gathering. As the caravan made its way into the midst of the crowd of marchers, these intruders began shouting racial insults from their car windows.

The crowd responded by beating on the intruders' cars and then trading blows with them. When a shot was fired from the car leading the caravan, the violence escalated. Some of the Nazis and Klansmen leapt out, pulling several loaded weapons from the trunk of one of their cars. At close range, they shot and killed five of the leading organizers and wounded ten other marchers.

Then they returned to their cars, stowed their weapons, and fled the scene. The media recorded much of this murderous action on videotape. It was being observed a couple of blocks distant by police officers, who had followed the Klan-Nazi caravan to the scene of the shootings but (in the absence of their tactical squad) did nothing to prevent the massacre.

When I heard the news on the radio and later saw videotaped footage of the shootings, it was scarcely believable to me. The next day I learned that one of our church officers, a funeral director, had courageously received the bodies of four of the murdered labor organizers and was in charge of the funeral arrangements for them. He was greatly agitated by the turmoil in the city, which put most of his personnel and equipment at considerable risk.

No one knew what might happen during the funeral. The National Guard had been called out and the city was in a near panic. Knowing the funeral director's fears, I offered to ride with him in the procession, and he gratefully accepted the offer. It was a nerve-wracking event, but it was completed without further violence. A tragic, unforgettable moment in Greensboro's history and mine.

Meanwhile, my work at the Church of the Covenant was proving very demanding, because of our steady loss of younger members to Presbyterian churches in suburban neighborhoods as well as dramatic changes in the church's neighborhood on the edge of downtown. The area around the church was now filled with transient college students and a few, mostly poor, aging neighbors. There were also growing numbers of homeless people, who frequented and occasionally camped on and sometimes abused the church property, making the members nervous.

Soon after my arrival as pastor, several members and I began reaching out to the variety of neighbors around the church, visiting with them in their homes or on the street and inviting them to join us. We opened a day care center for children of married students and other young families nearby. We also housed a Presbyterian counseling service for the city and welcomed Alcoholics Anonymous and Narcotics Anonymous groups to meet at the church. With Presbytery help and the leadership of our gifted young associate pastor, Frank Dew, Church of the Covenant sponsored a new congregation that shared our facilities: New Creation Community Presbyterian Church, of which Frank then became pastor. This small, somewhat experimental, deeply committed and racially integrated congregation brought new life and hope to us all.

In 1982, at Easter, my family and I suffered a terrible loss. Digie, my mother, a much-loved member of the church, died after years of declining health. Hers had been a life rich in service to her family, to the church, and to generations of children who knew her as a piano teacher and friend. The saints at Church of the Covenant were a great comfort to my family and to me in our loss.

Many months later, I attended a meeting of local clergy called by Henry Atkins, the Episcopal campus minister at the University of North Carolina-Greensboro. Henry had visited and befriended Nelson Johnson when Nelson was jailed after the November 3 massacre. Nelson, the chief organizer of the rally that day, was wounded and then arrested for expressing his outrage toward the police when they belatedly arrived on that bloody scene. Afterwards, he had been blamed and vilified by the Greensboro establishment and its media for what happened on November 3.

But when I met Nelson at the ministers' meeting, I found myself deeply impressed by his candid and remarkably gracious reflections on the massacre. His comments about it, and about the city's self-serving version of it—as reported by the local media and often repeated by the city's leaders in defense of their police—made far more sense to me than the media stories, or the Greensboro Police report of the event, or the U.S. Civil Rights Commission's investigative conclusions, or the report of the Greensboro Human Relations Commission. I had secured all of these documents from City Hall and studied them with some care and puzzlement. So I was most grateful for the cogency and spirit of Nelson's remarks.

I learned later that after the massacre Nelson had reclaimed his Christian heritage, which had earlier been overshadowed by his long-standing commitment to social and economic justice and had led to his Marxist associations. When I was told still later that he was attending a theological seminary and intended to be a Christian minister, I was not surprised. A few years after that, subsequent to Nelson's entry into the ministry, we encountered each other again at a ministers' meeting called to deal with Greensboro's neglected racial problems.

After that meeting, the two of us agreed to work together in an effort to establish a biracial group to address these matters. Working with us was one of the pastors of the First Presbyterian Church, Barbara Dua, who shared our community concerns. As a result of our combined efforts and those of numerous others who joined with us, the Beloved Community Center was formed. Under the leadership of Nelson, and later, his exceptionally gifted wife, Joyce Johnson, the BCC soon began to have a strong impact on Greensboro.

In 2001 the Beloved Community Center, along with the Greensboro Justice Fund—which was established by survivors of the November 3, 1979 massacre—joined with the International Center for Transitional Justice in initiating the Greensboro Truth and Community Reconciliation Project. As chair of the BCC Board of Directors at that time, I agreed to serve with our former mayor, Carolyn Allen, and with Rev. Gregory Headen, pastor of Greensboro's Genesis Baptist Church, as co-chairs of the Local Task Force.

Inspired by the work of other truth commissions, particularly South Africa's, with a National Advisory Group we designed a process of truth seeking for the sake of healing and community reconciliation for Greensboro. This led to the establishment of the Greensboro Truth and Reconciliation Commission, the first large-scale effort of its kind to be organized in this country. Denied the support of most of Greensboro's established leaders, we pressed on, developing a grassroots base and seeking the support of the city's religious leadership.

This Truth and Reconciliation process put us in touch with, and offered encouragement to, other communities suffering from unacknowledged truths and responsibilities related to events similar to our Greensboro Massacre: events such as Wilmington, North Carolina's "race riot" of 1898; Rosewood, Florida's "massacre" of 1923; and other tragic, unresolved incidents in the history of our country. It also put us in touch with truth commissions from as far away as Peru, South Africa, Sri Lanka and Northern Ireland—connections that have proved beneficial to all concerned.

Working with Nelson and Joyce Johnson in these far-reaching projects related to God's purpose of "beloved community for all" has enriched my life and enabled me to touch the lives of many others whom I could not otherwise have known. Since my retirement in 1993, working with the Beloved Community Center has become my ministry to the whole community, as R. Murphy Williams' ministry had been during his days at the Church of the Covenant. Through our various struggles in the interest of racial and economic justice, Nelson and I have become best of friends. He and his brilliant wife, Joyce, are astonishingly gifted and compassionate servant leaders whom I have come to love and to trust deeply as partners in the service of God and of the sort of beloved and loving community to which God calls us through Jesus, the servant of all.

By 2006 the Greensboro Truth and Reconciliation Commission had held numerous public hearings and personal interviews with key witnesses related to the 1979 massacre. The witnesses included Klansmen and Nazis, the widows and other survivors of those who were murdered, participants in the criminal and civil trials that had followed the event, residents of the neighborhood where the killings happened, and others directly affected by the 1979 massacre and its aftermath. At the end of its investigations, the Commission published an exceptionally fair and complete report of its findings, along with recommendations for steps toward healing the open wounds left by the tragedy and effecting the sort of community reconciliation that had been envisioned for the Truth and Community Reconciliation Process.

We who served on the Local Task Force of this project have recently been developing strategies for taking full advantage of the Commission's report and its recommendations in order to heal the lingering effects of the tragedy of November 3, 1979. We hope to move toward becoming a city in which all citizens are respected and empowered to develop their unique gifts and realize their potential for helping us become the beloved community which we believe God intends for us to be.

It hasn't been easy getting Greensboro to revisit and admit the failures of 1979 (see "Plea to the Christian People of Greensboro" in Appendix 3). Such pleas seem to have had little effect on prevailing attitudes of most members in the city's established churches and among the city's established leaders. And yet small but growing numbers from these groups have supported our efforts, God bless 'em! And God bless the nay-sayers as well! We remain hopeful for everybody as we press on.

The Truth Commission's splendid report is an excellent tool for educating generations of college and high school students in the unacknowledged workings of the systems of domination, denial, and repression that have corrupted our American experience and our city's life. Our American unwillingness to face up to the full measure of evils that have sullied our history from the beginning has taken on virulent forms that threaten not only this nation's future but that of the world and of life on this planet. We are in a heap of trouble. So we dare to hope that our truth process and its report can be useful in helping our own and other communities awaken to truths that, once faced and dealt with fairly and honestly, can free us for a more just and hopeful future.

Admittedly, our pursuit of such educational work and the changes implied by it may well make the established powers of today even more nervous and repressive than their predecessors were in 1979. But it also has the potential of helping open the eyes and minds—even the hearts—of future generations to new possibilities of honest and respectful resolution of differences, or even to repentance, forgiveness all around, and reconciliation within our community. It has strengthened my confidence and my trust in the way of Jesus, which I intend to continue following, come what may, in the days ahead. The biblical interpretations in this volume are offered in that spirit.

A Summary of the Contents

THE PASSAGES INTERPRETED IN this collection deal with critical moments and teachings of Jesus' liberating ministry, which reveal the prophetic spirit of his work and set the stage for understanding its painful, yet victorious outcome.

Chapter 1: The Beginning of the Gospel: John's Bad News. What feels like bad news—John's prophetic call to his people to repent of their sins and be baptized—is "the beginning of the good news of God." Jesus embraces John's call, is baptized, and then proceeds to embody the good news for which John's prophetic work has prepared the way.

Chapter 2: Jesus' Temptations—and Ours. After his baptism, Jesus, filled with the Holy Spirit, retreats to the desert where he rejects as demonic three tempting ways of attracting public acclaim and support for the good news which he is committed to proclaim. He then undertakes the tasks of embodying his radical message in his own unique way.

Chapter 3: Jesus Enrages the Home Folks. In the synagogue of Nazareth, his hometown, Jesus delights the congregation by announcing God's "good news to the poor," which is for all sorts of society's victims. But when he reveals that this good news also applies to the Gentiles, the enraged home folks try to kill him and he has to make a quick escape.

Chapter 4: "Let Us Go Across to the Other Side." Jesus leads his disciples in a dangerous crossing to the "other side" (the Gentile side) of the lake of Galilee. This is the sort of evangelical venture into enemy territory that was implied in his earlier remarks that so infuriated the home folks in Nazareth.

Chapter 5: Jesus' Tough Love. A rich young man approaches Jesus and asks what he must do to "inherit" eternal life. Jesus is touched, loves this seeker, but tells him he must first go, sell his property and give the proceeds to the poor, and then come, and follow him. Shocked and grieving, the young man turns and goes away.

Chapter 6: A Crooked Manager? Jesus tells a puzzling parable about a manager of a rich man's estate who is about to be fired. The manager, unwilling to become a worker, secures his uncertain future by having his master's poor debtors cut their IOU's in half, hoping for their help after he's fired.

Chapter 7: Community-building Economics. This subversive story, related to Israel's experience of the manna in the wilderness (Exodus 16), depicts a generous employer who pays all of his laborers what they need, rather than what they have earned. This generosity offends the workers who had worked longer hours and expected more. So the good news of God's concern for the welfare of all subverts ordinary economic assumptions and practices.

Chapter 8: Jesus Speaks to the "Neighbor Problem." Equally subversive of ordinary attitudes and values are the implications of Jesus' teachings about love. His parable of the "Good Samaritan" opens his hearers' eyes and hearts to alienated neighbors whose needs to be loved and served are to be taken as seriously as their own.

Chapter 9: A Call to Live Jesus' "Impossible Possibility." To his hearers who are oppressed by their own leaders and by their Roman overlords, in a society on the verge of exploding in bloody revolution, Jesus preaches love for outright enemies. This, he says, is God's way.

Chapter 10: A Prince of Peace Who Disturbs Our Peace? Jesus' socializing among, and identification with, society's outcasts—along with his radical teaching and practice of God's utterly inclusive love—make him a disturber of cheap "peace," as well as a cause of division within families and discouragement among his followers.

Chapter 11: Tempted to Cop Out? Pray Always! Jesus encourages his disciples not to lose heart in the face of the growing opposition they encounter as followers of their leader, whose way of all-inclusive love enrages the authorities of their society. Then he tells them a parable that underlines his teaching of perseverance in prayer.

Chapter 12: Jesus' Lonesome Valley—and Ours. As the end nears, the crowds of followers and the disciples themselves, except for a few courageous women, do "lose heart," and Jesus is left alone at the mercy of the authorities whom he has offended. Refusing to defend himself, he walks his "lonesome valley" to his death on the cross, having called his followers to take up their cross and follow in his loving, nonviolent way.

Chapter 13: A Vulnerable, Suffering God. Jesus' enemies, with the help of Judas' betrayal and the complicity of Pilate, the Roman governor, see to Jesus' arrest and crucifixion. He dies with a prayer of abandonment on his lips: his final revelation of God's vulnerable, suffering love.

Chapter 14: Jesus' Resurrection Makes All the Difference. Before Jesus was raised from the dead, the movement he started was thoroughly discredited, its leader disgraced, dead, and buried. But God raised Jesus from the grave, revealing the transforming significance of this death and vindicating his generous life. The resurrection made all the difference!

Chapter 15: Jesus' Way With the Alienated. Never once did Jesus use the victimized crowds that followed him to build a power base, or make a name for himself, or otherwise seek the sort of influence and control that kept the alienated masses down. His was the way of service, love, and empowerment of all for service in God's Beloved Community of peace on earth.

Chapter 16: About Our Meetings With Jesus. In saying to Nicodemus "You must be born from above," Jesus is inviting this follower, as he invites all of his followers, to receive the gift of a new life of freedom that is ruled not by the opinions and expectations of others but by God—empowered by the Holy Spirit to be free as Jesus was free.

Chapter 17: Surprised? The blessed people who inherit the eternal kingdom of God are those who seek and serve the welfare, dignity, and salvation of those who are degraded and rejected by others. Why blessed? Because Jesus, the Judge of all, is forever identified with these "least brothers and sisters" whom the world discounts and despises.

Chapter 18: Does It Still Make Sense? In the person of Jesus, the divine reality that fills and orders the universe is concentrated in a mortal human life. Everything that makes sense, all that gives beauty and order and meaning to life, was embodied in the life of this brother of us all. Jesus is no less than "God in the flesh." So yes, his story still makes sense!

Chapter 19: God Frees Us for Beloved Community. God's desire, as Jesus embodied it, is a community in which there are no first- and second-class members, and no expendables—a beloved and loving community in which all are equally loved by God, and all equally called to love God and to love and forgive one another as freely and generously as they themselves had been loved and forgiven.

The Beginning of the Gospel: John's Bad News

Luke 3:1–20

THE GOSPEL IS THE "good news" of God's grace: God's astonishing love for us embodied in Jesus Christ. But the beginning of that good news, according to all four of the biblical Gospels, is the ministry of John the Baptist. In response to his proclamation of a baptism of repentance for the forgiveness of sins, Jesus went out into the wilderness with the crowds, to be baptized by John.

Luke gives us the fullest picture of what John was up to out there. And frankly, it doesn't sound much like good news. To the crowds that came out to be baptized, John said:

> *You brood of vipers! Who warned you to flee from the wrath to come? Bear fruits worthy of repentance. Do not begin to say to yourselves, 'We have Abraham as our ancestor;' for I tell you, God is able from these stones to raise up children to Abraham. Even now the ax is lying at the root of the trees; every tree therefore that does not bear good fruit is cut down and thrown into the fire.*

That sounds to me like very *bad* news. And yet all four Gospel writers agree that John's ministry is, as Mark introduces it, "the beginning of the *good news* of Jesus Christ, the Son of God." So what are we to make of John's bad news here at the beginning of the good news?

In looking for light on that question, let's begin by reflecting a bit on the meaning of the "grace of God" which is the heart of the gospel message. According to Jesus' teaching, God is like a father who (to use one of our family expressions) is "just wild about his children." God is like the parent whose love never cools or disappears when the kids prove ungrateful or selfish, or because they foolishly get into trouble. Like such a parent,

God goes on loving prodigal, disobedient children and keeps on doing everything possible to help them grow up and realize their potential. It is this indestructible, undeserved love of God that we have in mind—or should have in mind—when we speak of God's grace.

The problem with the concept of God's grace is that we in the church, especially those of us who preach and teach, often give the impression that "the grace of God" is a sort of sentimental, undemanding goodness that we church folks are encouraged to "believe." Once we are on the record as believers, we are expected to be good church members, to support the church's programs and attend worship at regular intervals but otherwise get on with the business of our lives pretty much as before, except more honorably. When we mess up, God, who is gracious, will forgive; that's God's business.

This is the flabby kind of grace that Dietrich Bonhoeffer, who was martyred by the Nazis during World War II, exposed as "cheap grace." It was this notion of God's grace that was allowing German Christians to go along with Hitler's grandiose schemes for conquest in Europe, as well as the systematic persecution and elimination of Jews, Gypsies, Blacks, homosexuals and other unpopular minority groups. According to Bonhoeffer:

> Cheap grace means grace sold on the market . . . at cut prices. Grace is represented as the Church's inexhaustible treasury, from which she showers blessings with generous hands, without asking questions or fixing limits . . . In such a Church the world finds a cheap covering for its sins; no contrition is required, still less any real desire to be delivered from sin . . . Grace alone does everything . . . and everything can remain as it was before . . . The world goes on in the same old way.[1]

When one reflects on John the Baptist's scorching sermon to the "snakes fleeing from the wrath to come," it is hard to resist the conclusion that he saw the crowds he was addressing as victims of "cheap grace." And I think it's fair to say that they were. The religious symbol of their version of cheap grace was the messianic hope of Israel. We know that many believing Jews of that period shared the fervent hope that the God of their ancestors would send them a great king—the Messiah—who, by God's power, would deliver them from all their enemies. Then they, as the heirs of God's covenant promises, would take center stage and inherit the kingdom and power and glory that the world had so long denied them.

This hope had a variety of forms, but the fundamentals were rather constant. The Jews were God's people, heirs of God's promise of a Messiah from the line of David, who would finally secure their glorious inheritance for them. They believed that inheritance was theirs virtually by right of birth, because they were the children of Abraham.

A similar confidence is often expressed by Christians when we discuss differences among the Christian denominations. Someone will try to dispel the tension by saying, "Well, those things don't really matter all that much, because we're all going to the same place anyway." And if there's somebody like me around, they may add, hopefully, "Aren't we, preacher?" I take them to mean, "What matters is that we're all Christians by the grace of God, and we're all going to heaven."

But back to John the Baptist. John was a prophet. Not by birth, mind you. By birth John was a priest, a member of the Jewish establishment. But Luke tells us that "the word of God came to John . . . in the wilderness." That is, John received a prophetic call; he was irresistibly caught up in what God was doing in those days. He had been appointed to tasks he couldn't refuse and given a message that at all costs he must deliver. So John appeared in the desert, a setting like the site of Israel's purging after the escape from Egypt. And there, he began to preach with passion, like the prophets of old—calling all the people to repentance and baptism for the forgiveness of their sins in preparation for the coming judgment and the advent of the Messiah.

Not surprisingly, the excited multitudes flocked to him, full of nationalistic Jewish hopes. It was because he knew what was on their minds that John cried, "Who warned you to flee from the wrath to come—like snakes scurrying out of the way of a brush fire! Don't start saying to yourselves, 'We have Abraham for our father,' for I say to you that God is able from these stones to raise up children to Abraham."

John was saying that judgment was coming on the world, as his people hoped; but it wasn't to be God's judgment on those "bad people out there"—sinners, Gentiles, and outcasts—but on all people. Being a descendant of Abraham would be of no advantage whatever, because God would show no favoritism. John was accepting no excuses, no protestations of innocence, no blaming of others.

The devout were inclined in those days to blame others for the delay of the Messiah's coming, teaching that if all Israel would just keep the Law (as they themselves presumably did) for even one day, God's kingdom would immediately come. But John would have none of this. All were to turn to God: to repent and receive forgiveness for their sins. For no one was righteous in God's eyes. No exceptions.

What a shock! It was as though some radical, prophetic character would suddenly appear and say to us, "You scared rabbits; who warned you to run to church to try to escape the consequences of the way you've been living? Can't you see that your only hope lies in turning your lives around, trusting in God and starting all over like any new convert? Don't start saying to yourselves, 'But we're already Christians and members of a mainline denomination with a great heritage.' For I tell you, God can raise up from the streets of this city people for the church. If you are serious about repentance—about turning to God—then take this baptism of repentance seriously and show your sincerity by changing the way you have been living."

And maybe, since the hope that John was dealing with was not only religious and individualistic, but also nationalistic and communal, he might have to add for us American Christians, something like: "Don't start saying to yourselves, 'We are a Christian nation with great democratic institutions and with liberty and justice for all—not like our unbelieving detractors.' For I tell you, God can raise up among the poor in this country and in the Third World people who will truly cherish liberty and justice for all and carry the banner of human rights and human dignity among the nations. So if you intend to claim the name 'Christian,' then show it: bear the fruits of the Spirit of Jesus in your national and international affairs."

Such is the kind of leveling of the playing field that is the beginning of the good news. Now granted, it inevitably sounds like bad news to victims of cheap grace who have come to think that God's grace matters little in the "real world"—except to bless our special privileges and high living and ensure our entry into heaven by and by. For those of us who are content with going to church when it suits and otherwise continuing in our own self-centered ways—as though God is somehow obligated to bless us above others just because we are related to the church—John's kind of message will always appear to be bad news. At least at first. But the good news in this kind of bad news is that God does passionately care what kind of lives we live—all of us—regardless of who our mamas and daddies were or what gifts our culture and our particular situation in life have bestowed on us.

Well, John's shocked hearers apparently "got" that message. For they asked John—wringing their hands, as I picture it—"What then shall we do?" His answer to them was remarkably modest. He told those among the people who had two coats to share with those who were without, and instructed those who had food to spare to share with those who had none. He told the tax collectors, whose game was extortion (collecting more than people owed and pocketing the rest)—to collect no more than their due. And he told the occupation troops in the crowd to quit abusing their authority and to be content with their wages (accepting no payoffs or bribes was the point). In other words, John said in effect, "Quit going along with a corrupt system and milking it for your own benefit in ways that hurt vulnerable people."

It's so basic, so obvious; nothing new, nothing dramatic. Yet those simple, subversive words, if we heed them, can turn our way of life inside out. They will likely subvert some of our holiday plans—opening our hearts in new ways to include the forgotten ones of our society. They will surely call us back to the sort of simplicity and quiet listening that will enable us to hear what God is trying to say to us in the midst of all our shopping and other rushing about.

John's subversive instructions to folks like us, who are scrambling to accumulate more than we need, ought to be shouted from our steeples and enacted in the lives of penitent Christians all over this land, don't you think? For we who have been blessed with freedom and plenty for so long find it hard to imagine how oppressed, impoverished people feel; how they long for respect and self-determination and the necessities of a decent life. I'm sure John would, if he were here today, urge us to find respectful, empowering ways to share our freedom and abundance with the poor—the poor of our own communities and the suffering poor all over the world.

And finally, as John called on the tax collectors and soldiers to stop abusing their economic and military power over others, he would call us to do the same. He would admonish us to stop going along with and exploiting whatever special privileges our society accords us because of our race or class or gender. He would command us all to use such privileges in behalf of those who are denied them. I think he would also call on us as Americans to exercise our political responsibility by electing leaders who will quit abusing our nation's economic and political power in ways that exploit poor nations and their resources in order to support our habits of wasteful consumption.

What I see in John more clearly than ever before is this: John is God's prophetic spokesman for moral reality. He is a stubborn reminder to all Christian generations that there is no magical power of belief or birth that can relieve us of moral responsibility toward our neighbors and justice and integrity in our social relationships. Through the ages, John has stood at the gateway to God's new world: the "new creation" that God intended for us all in the gift of the beloved Son Jesus. John stands there in his strange desert garb, calling the generations to turn to God, calling on those who claim to be God's people to quit presuming that God owes us something special because of who we are or who our forebears were or what we "believe."

In the waning hours of the second millennium and at the dawn of the third, he calls us all to bear fruit worthy of repentance: to stop living in ways that make a mockery of our professions of faith and block the work that Jesus would do among us and through us in a time of great suffering and danger on our polluted planet. If the moral realism of his exposure of things that we would prefer to deny strikes us as bad news, then that's all the more reason to turn to God for the forgiveness God so urgently offers us, and to claim the good news that our lives and our world need not continue the way they are heading.

Long after his baptism by John, Jesus spoke to the crowds around him, asking: "What did you go out into the wilderness to look at? A reed shaken by the wind?" (i.e., blowing this way and that, according to the latest opinion polls)." What then did you go out to see? Someone dressed in soft robes? Look, those who put on fine clothing and live in luxury are in royal palaces. What then did you go out to see? A prophet?" Jesus answered his own questions: "Yes, I tell you, and more than a prophet . . . I tell you, among those born of women no one is greater than John; yet the least in the kingdom of God is greater than he" (Luke 7:24b–26, 28).

The good news in John's bad news is that we are not obliged to go along with the spirit and the arrangements of the world as it is. We are called to be a part of that "greater" community of love born of the Spirit of Jesus: a community in which there is room and love enough for all the hungry, broken, struggling children of God in the whole world. John's greatness is that he is the eternal preparer of the way of the Lord—Jesus' crazy cousin who reveals to us the embarrassing necessity of emptying our hearts of selfish, divisive hopes and turning to God. For only God can empower us for the subversive works of love that must finally overcome the power of evil in us and in our world.

ENDNOTES

1. Bonhoeffer, *The Cost of Discipleship*, 37.

2

Jesus' Temptations—and Ours

Luke 4:1–13

W̲E̲ F̲O̲L̲L̲O̲W̲E̲R̲S̲ O̲F̲ J̲E̲S̲U̲S̲ have peculiar temptations that are not easy to recognize as temptations. And that's because we have a peculiar mission. If we had a conventional mission—for example, to be successful promoters of a successful religious organization that would attract our kind of people—then I suspect that the temptations that Jesus faced, and that we must deal with as his followers, wouldn't seem like temptations at all. They would simply be considered sensible approaches to winning support for our cause.

But Jesus experienced them as temptations when he set out on his radical mission of demonstrating the will of God. He did so in the midst of a society that was so filled with anger, and disease, and poverty, and oppression that it would soon self-destruct in a devastating war. We, as his disciples, are called to carry forward Jesus' peculiar mission, under his leadership, in his Spirit, in times that are frighteningly like those that he faced.

Think how divided the human race is at this moment: rich against poor, nations and religious and ethnic groups choosing sides and threatening or terrorizing one another with every kind of weapon, including weapons of mass destruction. Our own nation, trying to dominate the world and its resources for the benefit of our corporations and consumers, is more divided and our politics more rancorous than at any other time I can remember. We're frustrated with one another, demonizing and blaming one another and the rest of the world for our troubles, while all of us live under the threat of a deteriorating environment and weapons that could end civilization as we know it.

In the midst of all this, we are called to carry on Jesus' world-transforming mission. And, God knows, the world is in desperate need of such transformation. This calling makes us vulnerable to the peculiar temptations Jesus faced—peculiar because they don't always seem like temptations but rather like necessary, workable ways to get an urgently important job done.

According to Luke, Jesus summed up his mission with these words from Isaiah:

> *The Spirit of the Lord is upon me,*
> *because he has anointed me*
> *to bring good news to the poor.*
> *He has sent me to proclaim*
> *release to the captives*
> *and recovery of sight to the blind,*
> *to let the oppressed go free,*
> *to proclaim the year of the Lord's favor.* (Luke 4:18–19)

Those of us who claim to be Jesus' followers today are *to bring good news to those who are being crushed by poverty*. And that's a majority of the human race, including millions of our neighbors in the U.S.A. We are also *to proclaim release to the captives*. This includes not only rehabilitation and freedom for the inmates in our crowded prisons, but also liberation for neighbors captive to drink, or drugs, or greed, or lust, or abusive control, or their own fears and prejudices.

We are *to offer recovery of sight to the blind*, including not only those who physically can't see, but also those who *won't see* because they don't want to see the truth about their own lives or the crying needs of their neighbors. Like Jesus, we are *to help the oppressed go free*, including those who are suffering in abusive relationships at home, or at work, or anywhere else in our own society, as well as those who are being crushed by dictators, and police states, and greedy corporations, and warring factions all over the world.

We are *to proclaim and embody the time of the Lord's favor*: JUBILEE! This is God's general amnesty for all offenders, including us: forgiveness and restoration for all the broken, alienated, confused members of the human family (See Leviticus 25:8–17).

What could be more peculiar, more countercultural, than such a mission as this in our conflicted world?

Such an extraordinary message and mission demands extraordinary methods of those who are called to fulfill it. Ordinary methods just won't do, because ordinary methods are what have gotten the world into the mess it's in. This story depicting Jesus' struggle with temptation pictures his rejection of the familiar means used to promote causes and attract followings. It is told here by Luke for the sake of all of those, including you and me, whom Jesus calls to join him in his extraordinary mission.

As we look for the meaning of this story, it's important to remember that this is an imaginative presentation of a mental and spiritual experience, not a factual report of actual conversations between Jesus and a "Tempter." Jesus would have used it to inform his disciples of the struggles of his own soul as he wrestled with the issue of how to use the power of life and love that God had given him for the carrying out of God's mission. So the actual situation on which it is based is Jesus, alone, in the desert, fasting, reflecting, praying, struggling over a strategy for his work; not Jesus miraculously flying from place to place in the company of a demon with horns and a pitchfork.

Jesus' first, and probably our own most persistent, temptation is to focus on bread: bread in the sense of the necessities of physical existence. The Tempter's proposition, related to our own situation, might go something like this:

> So you "children of God" want to reach people with your good news? Then remember this: whose bread they eat, his song they will sing. Be realistic. You can talk your theology to 'em until you're blue in the face, but the one who controls their bread wins the arguments in this world. You've got to give 'em good news that they can see and touch and taste.
>
> When people are hungry, talk about God and faith will fly right by them. But if you show people you can turn stones into bread for them—I mean, make them more prosperous and comfortable, more secure materially and financially—then you've got 'em. They'll say AMEN to whatever you say, and maybe even do what you want them to do.
>
> Remember: the promise of more bread is what gives global capitalism its power over you and over the lives and imaginations of struggling people all over the world today. So don't be stupid. Use it! Use it to promote your gospel, to get people to church, to get the power you need to make the world a better place.

How are we to respond to this devilish commonsense proposition? First, by remembering, as our Leader did, that "human beings don't live by bread alone." Which is to say, bread is not the sole source of our lives. God, who gives us bread—and who, if we pay attention, will show us what to do with it—is the source and sustainer of our lives. We are to use our "bread-making power" as Jesus used his—not in order to manipulate others or for personal satisfaction. People's need for physical survival is not to be used to enrich us at the expense of others or to gain power over others, but to make life good and bountiful for all.

Furthermore, the focus of our mission is not on bread *as bread*. Our peculiar mission is not to promise people that we can satisfy their desires and appetites. For example: "If you join our church, it will be good for your business"; or, "This is where you can meet the right people"; or, "Come on and join us—we have a great facility, beautiful sanctuary, marvelous organ, outstanding choir, excellent child care, and the best church suppers in town!"

Jesus recognized that if he focused on the material benefits of faith, that would obscure people's deeper needs and leave them as selfish and competitive and vulnerable to greed and self-seeking as they were before they heard the gospel. Jesus' concern was that our souls be nourished on the spiritual bread of God's love and forgiveness. This is what can free us from anxiety over food and shelter and the other necessities of life. Free us to quit the endless "rat race" for more stuff. Free us to experience the joy of sharing what we do have with those who desperately need it, in a world where 40,000 children die every day for lack of nourishing food.

To set up the second of our peculiar temptations, the Tempter shows us a panoramic view of all the nations that Jesus wanted to reach, and wants us to reach. Then he whispers to us, as he whispered to Jesus:

So you "children of God" want to reach everybody with your good news? Okay, take a good look at that world—the real world out there. Then let's get one thing clear: Mine is the "invisible hand" in charge of this world, regardless of what you may have heard in church. So if you are going to reach people religiously in my world, you'll do it my way. Or if you want me to put that in religious terms, you sell them on worship and church activities by approaching them in my spirit.

Appeal to their vanity and their everlasting desire to be more right, more godly than other people. Manipulate their religious and political prejudices. Get celebrities to endorse your programs. And keep them comfortable. I know people, and I know what works. Do as I say, and I guarantee, you can build the biggest, most admired, best publicized, most generously endowed "superchurch" of them all.

Just remember, this is not "heaven"; this is the "real" world of here and now, where my way works. *Trust me. Don't trust some invisible "God"—because in this world, my world, the winners do things my way.*

How would Jesus have us respond to these claims of old "Worldly Wisdom," who confuses himself with God? Jesus says, "It is written, 'You shall worship the Lord your God, and serve God alone.'"

That's straight talk, friends. Our peculiar mission is first of all to trust God, and God alone—here and now, and forever. Trusting in God, we are to engage in the liberating work of overcoming the terrible injustices of society, of subverting the barriers of race and class, and of religion and politics and sexual orientation—all the differences used by greedy power mongers to set us against one another and thwart God's purpose of a human community that's united in prayer and mutual respect, honest speech and honest dealings. United in God's love, which includes everybody.

But friends, when we, who are supposed to be engaged in this extraordinary mission, instead put our trust in the ordinary self-justifying "tricks" that "work" in the market places and the political and military arenas of our society—and even use that stuff to try to get what we want in church—then we are engaged in devil worship, not Christian mission. We are to love God with all the passion of our being, freed by God to surrender our selfish ambitions and prejudices and all the shady tricks available to us. We are to trust God alone with the outcome of our lives and our mission, as Jesus did. *That* is our proper worship

So we come to our third peculiar temptation. This scenario is set in Jerusalem, the center of the Jewish world and of Jewish imagination. In fact, it's set at the center of that center: the very pinnacle of the temple. What a marvelous place for "making a statement," as we say these days. Like the dome of the Capitol in D.C. on Inauguration Day!

Right there at the center of the center, the Tempter (as I imagine it) grins, throws up his hands, starts to walk away, and over his shoulder shouts:

All right, I give up. You win! But if you are so determined to trust God, then you'd better make sure that God will bail you out when people reject your naive efforts, which they will; I know 'em.

Before you go way out on your prophetic limb, speaking the "plain truth" to people who are accustomed to more nuanced messages, and the powers that be cut that limb off behind you—well, you had better make sure God will catch you when you fall. So jump. And let God show 'em you really are his Son. After all, your scripture says, "God will command his angels to protect you . . . On their hands they will bear you up, lest you dash your foot against a stone." (Psalm 91:11–12)

And what's Jesus' response when old Temptation starts quoting scripture at him, to get him to prove how very special and how very right he is to trust God; and how God is therefore absolutely obligated to take very special care of him? Jesus simply quotes scripture right back at the pious old devil: "You don't put the Lord God to the test," he says. God is to be *trusted,* not *tested.*

The point is, God's servants are not called to be religious heroes and celebrities. We are simply called to be faithful to our peculiar mission. While on that mission, we are not promised exemption from the dangers and sorrows that befall others. On the contrary, as followers of Jesus, we are to be prepared for the extra pain inflicted on us by people who are so captive to enslaving evil that they can't believe the good news; who can't face the truth of their need, and who therefore fight against its messengers.

Our task is to bring the world the gospel of God's indiscriminate love, claiming it not only for ourselves but for *everybody*— especially the marginal, broken, unpopular folk who are being most flagrantly denied love and justice by society and its leaders. You can't deliver Jesus' kind of subversive message without expecting to get into trouble with the exploiters and oppressors of society.

As Jesus plainly said elsewhere, if any would follow in his way, they must deny themselves the luxury of safety and take up their cross. They must face the murderous reactions of the established powers against those who resist their control. Face their hostility and endure it for the sake of justice and healing for *all.* Jesus knew that disciples of his who cling to their lives, always seeking safety and security behind their ego defenses, will lose their chance at life. While those who lay their lives on the line for the sake of the gospel will find life abundant and eternal.

Luke tells us that, "When the devil had finished every temptation, he departed from Jesus *until an opportune time.*" And there were many such times for Jesus. As there are for us.

Remember when Peter tried to turn Jesus aside from his conviction that his mission would lead him through suffering, rejection, and death? "Far be all that from you, Lord!" declared Peter. And how did Jesus deal with that "opportune moment" of temptation? Without hesitating, he turned on Peter with the words, "Get behind me, *Satan*! You're not think-ing like God but like a man"—and a tempter at that! (Mark 8:31–33)

Another such moment occurred in the wilderness when the crowds whom he had fed wanted to make Jesus a king, then and there. It was an "opportune moment" for him to quit trusting God and grab for power to silence his enemies. But he would have none of it.

In both of these "opportune moments," it was Jesus' friends who took the Tempter's role. And so it is often with us. The most urgent and powerful temptations can come to us from the mouths of friends and loved ones concerned "for our own good" because we seem to them to be taking Jesus' way too seriously. Likewise, the most diabolical temptations often come to our churches through the lips of those concerned for the "good reputation" and "positive image" of the church—as when we are discussing opening the church and its buildings to unpopular people and causes.

Beloved, the fact is, there is an evil spirit abroad in the world—a lying, tempting spirit of domination and rationalization, which crouches at the door of our hearts, awaiting opportune moments. That spirit of "life as usual" regularly turns people away from God and against one another. And that spirit can seduce us into exchanging our life-giving mission for some sort of worldly success. Which in the end is only a devilish cover for a betrayal of our Lord and of our mission and ourselves.

But such shameful defeats need not be. For Jesus has shown us in this amazing old story *a better way*: to live by the Word and will of God. To worship and serve God alone. And to trust God completely with the outcome of our mission and our lives. *We may be assured, God will never betray our trust.*

3

Jesus Enrages the Home Folks

Luke 4:14–30

L IKE MANY BELIEVERS, I first met Jesus through the stories told me in my childhood by those who loved him and loved me. From the beginning, I understood Jesus to be the Son of God, the Savior of the world. As such, he was pretty much removed from my experience—an exalted figure, larger than life, about whom we Christians believed mysterious things that were, frankly, hard for me to accept.

As I grew older, I found it increasingly difficult to embrace all that zealous Christian friends said we were supposed to believe and experience in relation to Jesus and the Bible. And yet I couldn't let Jesus go. Or rather, he wouldn't let me go.

As late as my years in seminary, Jesus' very human struggle was only beginning to break through the pious unreality that surrounded him in my mind. In fact, the truth of his humanity actually dawned on me after I had finished my preparation for ministry. I was in Scotland trying to write a doctoral dissertation on Jesus as God's servant.

One night I was reading *The Message of Jesus* by biblical scholar Martin Dibelius, who was trying to recover the original form of the stories about Jesus as they circulated orally among the early Christians in the decades before the gospel writers recorded them. Dibelius had lifted the sayings of Jesus and the stories about him from the gospels and grouped them according to their literary forms: the parables, the healing stories, the controversies with his critics, and so on. Dibelius had eliminated from them whatever in his judgment seemed secondary or editorial and had printed each saying or episode without the surrounding context of the gospel narrative—just the early church's vivid memories of Jesus' words and deeds.

The result was startling to me. I devoured those arresting sayings and stories one after another in rapid succession: Jesus' commandments, his healing assurances, his promises about the kingdom of God, and his challenge of everything he encountered that was hardhearted and phony and dead. As I read, I was deeply moved. His disturbing words and courageous acts captured my imagination and stripped my soul bare.

That reading about Jesus in an ice-cold Scottish attic set my heart and mind on fire. After that night, for better or worse, I was his. My main purpose in life ever since has been to open my heart and mind to Jesus' radical, life-changing message: to know him, to follow him, to be empowered by his Spirit to become like him, and to share him with others.

Jesus' vision of the kingdom of God shaped his life and presents an offer to shape ours as well. He was our poor brother who lived among poor people. He was a man who sought no honor or praise for himself. He was plain spoken, devoid of any hint of pomposity or lust for power and glory, unschooled in any sophisticated sense, yet aflame with the Spirit of God and consumed by a vision of God's will being done on this earth.

In Jesus' life and death is embodied the secret of who God is. If we consider his life from the standpoint of its outcome, we must ask, what was Jesus doing that caused the Romans to subject him to their cruelest punishment, a form of execution reserved for dangerous subversives and slaves? What was Jesus doing that caused the most respected religious leaders among his people to denounce him as a blasphemer and to join forces with the political authorities of his day to do away with him as a threat to the people's peace?

What caused the crowds who had earlier received his message so gladly to turn against him at the last and choose to save a terrorist's life instead of his? What was he doing that caused his closest friends to desert him and run for their lives in his moment of greatest need? What was Jesus up to that so frightened and offended all of them—except for a few courageous women—that that they abandoned him to a criminal's death, forsaken and alone?

The answer, I believe, is that Jesus was declaring and embodying the reign of God, that time when God's will would at last be done on this earth. This meant that he was calling his followers to an alternative way of life in God's beloved community, a way that was subversive of the religious, economic, and political world of their day. His call was to a new, all-embracing loyalty to God, a new way of living—not in some perfect apocalyptic future (in heaven "by and by"), but *here and now* in this violent, sinful world.

In Luke's report of Jesus' visit to his hometown synagogue in Nazareth, Jesus characterized his radical alternative in the words of the prophet Isaiah, as good news to the poor, release to the captives, recovery of sight to the blind, and liberation of the oppressed. In short, he was proclaiming God's great Jubilee: forgiveness and a new start for everybody—without exception! (See Leviticus. 25:8–17). And the home folks loved it. At first.

But then, Jesus began to spell out the implications of his message. He told his hearers that this good news—this end to slavery, imprisonment, and oppression—applied not only to them and their children but to everybody. *Really everybody.* Including the Gentiles, people they had been pleased to hate and blame for the troubles in their world. That was when the home folks became enraged, ran him out of town, and tried to kill him.

They might have succeeded, except that it was not yet Jesus' time. God willed more of Jesus' story to unfold before that fateful day on Calvary. There were more hearts to be touched, more minds to be challenged, more bodies to be healed, more consciences to be awakened, more controversies to be joined, more disciples to be called and trained to share and continue his mission.

But here, near the beginning of his narrative, Luke has revealed to us the heart of that mission: *Jesus came to bring good news to the poor.* And who were these poor? The pages of the gospels are filled with them.

They were, first of all, the beggars: the sick and disabled who were afflicted with blindness and leprosy and paralysis. They were essentially unemployable, many even untouchable according to Jewish law, and therefore often without anyone willing to support them. They were like the neediest, most troubled of today's poor and homeless people. They were that society's rejects, who could only cry out, "Jesus, have mercy on me!"

And he did. So they flocked to him full of hope that, here at last, was a leader who was on their side. And many were healed and empowered through his caring and encouragement." See, your faith has made you well," he proclaimed over the healed woman who had suffered from a hemorrhage (Matthew 9:22)—and perhaps over others who needed such affirmation.

Also among "the poor" to whom Jesus' message was such good news were children. In the society of Jesus' time, children were pawns in an adult world. Like too many children in our world today, they were subject in infancy to death by exposure or malnutrition, and as youngsters to being sold into slavery, unless their fathers (yes, fathers) wanted and blessed them. But to Jesus they were valued persons in their own right, to be loved and respected for their unique gifts.

Who could forget the story of his taking a little child, setting the child in the midst of his hearers, and declaring, "Truly I tell you, unless you change and become like children, you will never enter God's kingdom?" (Matthew 18:3) He affirmed children as our teachers simply by honoring the child's being: its openness to the future, its vulnerability and trust—qualities so needed in Jesus' followers.

Women also were among "the poor," for they were branded by their gender as inferior and hemmed in by many constricting rules and customs. It was deemed sinful to teach a woman the law, improper for a man to speak to, much less touch, a woman in public. But Jesus ignored such demeaning restrictions.

Consider the example of the woman who came in off the street one day and disrupted a dinner in a prominent Pharisee's home to which Jesus had been invited (Luke 7:36–50). She approached Jesus as he ate, washed his feet with her tears, dried them with her hair, kissed them, and anointed them with precious ointment—much to the embarrassment of Jesus' proper host, who felt offended by both Jesus and the woman. But was Jesus embarrassed, or apologetic? Not at all.

Instead, he affirmed the woman's courageous act of gratitude as a sign that she had been forgiven "many sins," in contrast to his host, whose attitude that day betrayed a heart that had been "forgiven little." So Jesus honored this woman of the street as the teacher that day at this prominent religious leader's home. The world has barely begun to recognize and to honor the implications of Jesus' good news to women and children, so long oppressed in a world of male domination.

The "sinful masses" of Jesus' world were also among "the poor" who were recipients of the good news." Sinners" was in fact a sort of technical term in Jesus' day, employed by devout believers to describe the great majority of their fellow Jews who, either because of their poverty and ignorance or the requirements of their livelihoods, did not or could not keep the Law of Moses. Poor, hardworking people simply couldn't observe all the dietary and ritual laws of cleanness and uncleanness, or even the Sabbath with all its regulations. So these "sinners" were looked down on by the pious and knowledgeable few, in much the same spirit that the homeless and the demoralized poor are looked down on by proper and prosperous religious folk these days.

Furthermore, such "sinners" (which meant the great majority of the population) were very much aware of their second-rate status. They believed that they were inferior to the scribes and Pharisees who had the inside track with God as teachers and keepers of the Law. They accepted that they were inferior to the Sadducees and priests who ruled the religious establishment and managed the temple, whom in their eyes God had blessed with great wealth and position.

They were the "multitude ignorant of the law" and therefore "accursed" in the eyes of the religious establishment. The label "sinners" was their fate and their shame, believed to be visited on them by God and confirmed at every turn by the more "righteous" minorities in power. In this respect too, they were very like our poor friends today whom the rest of us are self-righteously inclined to defame and blame for their poverty.

No wonder they flocked to John's baptism of repentance for forgiveness of sins, fleeing from "the wrath to come " (Luke 3:7). And no wonder they suffered from the kinds of infirmities of body and soul that people who feel degraded and guilty and frustrated by life so often suffer. But these were the very ones whom Jesus persistently identified with, welcomed, served, and healed. The healings of which we hear in our gospels are, above all else, acts of *inclusion* and *welcome* to outcasts who, because of their afflictions, were considered unclean, even untouchable. Jesus freely and repeatedly violated the law (especially the Sabbath and purity regulations) that set religious custom above the urgent needs of these suffering people.

All of the groups of "sinners" that I have described were the nobodies who ruined—or, rather *made*—Jesus' reputation, by accepting his friendship and embracing his message. "He's a glutton and a drunkard, a friend of tax collectors and sinners," complained his righteous critics when they saw him at table with these friends of his, breaking the rules of table fellowship that were so important in a world so conscious of religious and social status. And his response? "It is not the healthy who need a physician but those who are sick; I have come to call not the righteous but sinners" (Mark 2:15–17).

Other religious movements of the day called "the righteous," such as the strict, law-abiding Pharisees and the Essenes, who were stricter still, constantly bathing, studying, and praying in an effort to keep themselves pure of contamination. Even the Zealots, who were terrorists and revolutionaries, had their standards. They recruited stouthearted patriots who were always ready to strike a bloody blow for the liberation of Israel and the triumph of God's purpose as they understood it. All these movements gathered their exclusive factions from the ranks of the gifted and the committed and the devout—the "relatively righteous."

But not Jesus. Instead of gathering the respected and the devout, and separating them from the impoverished masses, he announced good news to the poor, the debased, and all those trapped in sin and despair—especially the most desperate. And he welcomed them *all*, lived with them, and served them.

It was so strange. So unexpected. So disturbing! *So revolutionary*! While others continued to draw lines of separation and steadfastly guarded the boundaries and power arrangements that alienated people from one another—the "righteous" from "sinners," the men from women and children, the rich from the poor, Jews from Gentiles, Pharisees from Sadducees, the "clean" from the "unclean," and on and on—Jesus was declaring a new family: the inclusive family of the merciful God whom Jesus knew as Abba, "Father." He was declaring and demonstrating that God's beloved community is open to all who would hear God's word of forgiveness and love for all and follow it.

Clearly, Jesus was offering God's gracious alternative to the whole social system of domination, exploitation, and division that was keeping the poor poor, keeping desperate sinners without hope, keeping the sick captive to their illnesses, the "possessed" enslaved by evil and the "righteous" and powerful trapped in their oppressive roles and blind to their own desperate need for repentance. Not that Jesus didn't care about the "righteous" and powerful. He loved them, engaged them, debated with them, ate with them on occasion, and had friends among them, such as Nicodemus and Joseph of Arimethea. But he never curried their favor or support; never tried to "sell" them on being his followers. And he was quite candid in exposing their need for repentance and changed lives.

Jesus' message and behavior were in radical contradiction to the values of the age and the society of his time. Or any time, for that matter. Ours especially included. So it is no wonder that his frightened, bewildered friends finally forsook him; that the crowds at the end deserted him; that his Nazarene home folks were enraged by his love for their enemies; and that his enemies were quick to do away with him as a dangerous social and religious revolutionary. A society captive to evil powers within and without had to silence this man—or repent—which required being radically changed, personally and institutionally.

To the end, Jesus remained true to the will of the One who had called him. With the prayer "Thy will be done" on his lips and in his heart, he walked calmly into the darkness and terror of crucifixion, while others conspired against him, or abandoned him, or ridiculed him in their pathetic efforts to extricate themselves from the power of his love and the threat of his message. Speaking for all of us, they were saying in their various ways, "No! This is too dangerous, too radical, too idealistic."

But God said, "Yes. YES! The future is his, for his is the way to life and community and healing for this suffering world."

Through it all, Jesus' fidelity to the poor and the outcast, and his identification with them in their suffering and forsakenness, never wavered. He was their companion in death as in life. He died in communion with all who suffer abandonment, pain, and death.

In Jesus we see God revealed, not as the almighty patron of believers, far removed from our moments of darkness and despair, but as the absolutely faithful fellow sufferer and companion of all our days, who will never forsake a single one of us broken, uncomprehending human beings, however tragic our sin and need.

In life and in death, Jesus challenged the world with a genuine, life-giving alternative to its divisive, destructive ways: God's beloved community. Through him you and I—indeed *all*—are invited to live this splendid alternative in the midst of our lonely, suffering world, knowing that Jesus is with us still. God with us in the midst of our struggle. With us to lead, to sustain, to bless, and to give us victory over all the powers of alienation and death.

Thanks be to God.

4

"Let Us Go Across to the Other Side"

Mark 4:35–41 and Jonah 1:1–17

Sitting in a boat at the edge of the lake, where he has been teaching, Jesus says to his disciples, "Let us go across to the other side." It sounds almost casual, as though he had decided they needed a break from dealing with the crowds. "Good thinking!" we might say. "They need some time for themselves; we all do." Unfortunately, this sort of modern interpretation would surely miss Mark's point in telling this story.

You may have heard the tale about the joke club whose members knew one another's jokes so well that they quit telling them and instead numbered them. Then, whenever a member thought a particular joke fit well at some point in the club meeting, he could simply shout out its number. And everyone would crack up laughing.

Of course, a puzzled outsider would completely miss the point. I think that we modern Christians who try to read and understand Mark's stories of Jesus are often like that. Unless we acquaint ourselves with the stories that were in the minds and experience of Mark's first-century readers, we will be puzzled outsiders who miss his point again and again.

So, what do we need to know of the experience of Mark and those for whom he wrote this story, that will help us to get the point? First of all, we need to recognize that Mark's story was not written about people like most of us. We Presbyterians and others of the so-called "mainline denominations" (God forgive us our arrogance) enjoy a reasonable measure of respectability, prosperity, and privilege in our society.

In contrast, throughout Mark's story, it is the poor people, along with others whom society excluded, who are Jesus' principal companions and his immediate concern. At the beginning, at his baptism, Jesus is with them. Not in the synagogue with the scribes, or in Jerusalem at the temple with the "important" people. But out in the wilderness, with the crowds—the masses—identifying with them in their need of God's forgiveness, and in their hope for a new world under the reign of God.

Ched Myers writes of Mark in *Binding the Strong Man*: "Throughout his narrative of Jesus' ministry the crowds are there, continually pursuing, interrupting, and prevailing upon him. Jesus' compassion is always first directed toward [these insistent] masses and their overwhelming needs and demands."[1] This is true right up to the end, when the Jerusalem authorities manage to manipulate the Passover crowds into clamoring for his execution.

According to Myers, Jesus' story as Mark tells it is in the most fundamental way their story: good news for the masses of ordinary people who were trying to cope with the daily realities of disease, poverty, and disenfranchisement that characterized the social existence of first-century Palestine's poor. For them, Jesus is a liberator, not in a disembodied, "spiritual" sense, but as a healer of their diseases and silencer of their demons—as their friend and champion in their struggle for dignity and inclusion in the community of God's people, Israel. Our relatively privileged experience is so very different from that of the people in Mark's stories, as well as the experience of those for whom he wrote, that we are apt to miss his point again and again, unless we constantly try to put ourselves in their place and read with ears attuned to their history, their stories, their fears and frustrations, and their hopes.

With this in mind, we return to Jesus' words, "Let's go across to the other side." What would those words have meant to his disciples? The "other side" refers here to the Gentile shore—as opposed to the Jewish side—of the lake that Mark calls the Sea of Galilee. Jesus is talking about crossing over into enemy territory!

This lake that they are about to cross is only about fifteen miles long and scarcely ten miles wide. So, why would Mark refer to a lake of that size as a sea, when others didn't? The answer lies in Israel's history, which is the background against which Mark writes his story. In the formative story of that history, the Exodus from Egypt, the Hebrew slaves were delivered from certain destruction at the Red Sea by God's opening up a way for them, then closing it down and drowning Pharaoh's pursuing troops.

Ever after their experience there, the sea was a powerful metaphor for the danger and distress from which God again and again delivered the faithful of Israel.

For example, we read in Psalm 107:27–29 that sailors in a tempest "cried to the Lord in their trouble, and he brought them out of their distress; he made the storm be still, and the waves of the sea were hushed." The Psalmist, whose conviction was imbedded in the minds of Mark's readers, is a silent interpreter of his story here.

Equally important for our understanding of this passage is the story of Jonah, which is paired with Mark's in the lectionary. Jonah's disaster at sea was a result of his response to God's calling him to be a missionary to Nineveh—"that bloody city," as one of the prophets styled it. Nineveh was the capital of Assyria, the cruelest and bloodiest of the aggressive Gentile neighbors that terrorized the little kingdoms of Israel.

Obviously, Jonah hated the very thought of being God's missionary to those unspeakable Ninevites. That's why he took the first available ship in the opposite direction. But according to the story, God was serious about this Assyrian mission, and sent a terrible storm on the sea, so that Jonah's ship was threatened with being broken apart. When the terrified sailors found Jonah down in the ship's hold where he was trying to sleep through the tempest, they rousted him out." What are you doing sound asleep?" they cried." Get up, call on your god! Perhaps the god will spare us a thought so that we do not perish."

At this point, Jonah "outed," as we say: He admitted that he was a Hebrew, who served the Lord who made the sea and the dry land. Hearing this, the sailors became even more terrified and demanded, "What is this that you have done?" (Jonah 1:6–10).

You can hear the resonance with Mark's story: the storm, the sailors' terror, Jesus asleep, their cry for help, and at the end their awestruck question, "Who is this . . . ?" Mark has obviously loaded his account with these echoes of the Jonah story to enable his readers to relate it to the church's dangerous and often stormy mission to the Gentiles. His telling of it reminds his readers of the dangers faced by Jesus' early followers. Apostles such as Paul and Silas and Peter and John obeyed Jesus' command to cross the great divide of hostility and misunderstanding that separated the Jewish from the Gentile worlds, for the sake of spreading to all the world the good news of the gospel.

To those early followers of Jesus who read Mark's Gospel, Jesus' invitation, "Let's go across to the other side," would have had the sort of chilling implications that an invitation to go along on an unauthorized trip to Soviet Russia would have had for us Americans at the height of the Cold War. Or that an invitation to go along on a street-preaching mission in one of the inner-city war zones of New York or Chicago or Los Angeles would likely have for us now.

When Jesus tells the disciples "Let's go across to the other side," he's not inviting them to take a little break for rest and relaxation from the pressures of the mission to their own people. He's calling them to press on to the more dangerous work of the kingdom, which breaches the terrible walls of fear and hostility that separated Jews from Gentiles as enemies: a gulf of hostility and misunderstanding and prejudice like those that separate all sorts of "enemies" in our divided world today. And that is what Jesus has been doing ever since.

I was in the ministry for many years before I learned that the words of Jesus most quoted by Christian writers during the first three centuries of the Christian era were these from Matthew: "Love your enemies and pray for those who persecute you, so that you may be children of your Father in heaven; for he makes his sun rise on the evil and on the good, and sends rain on the righteous and on the unrighteous" (Matthew 5:44–45). In our story from Mark, Jesus was simply acting out God's indiscriminate love by "going over to the other side" to deliver the good news to strangers and enemies.

On the basis of Jesus' love—which revealed God's love for everyone, including those deemed God's "enemies"—the early Christians renounced violence, war, and military service in their effort to bear witness to the good news intended even for those on "the other side." Such an attitude was unique in the ancient world, as it is in our day. For their fidelity to Jesus' command of love, along with their general unwillingness to put their allegiance to Rome above their allegiance to Jesus Christ, many of those early Christians were persecuted, and not a few, executed.

But after the Roman Emperor Constantine found it expedient to become a Christian in the fourth century, all this changed. The church began receiving preferential treatment from the Roman Empire, as it now does from the American Empire. It became respectable, even patriotic, to be a Christian.

Rome's hatred of its enemies—and Rome's wars, which had once seemed so evil—then appeared to many Christians to be just and necessary for preserving the gospel. The church began to bless Rome's wars the way most American Christians have blessed America's wars. Tragically, most of us Christians have accepted war and violence as necessary means of dealing with evil enemies, ever since that tragic departure from Jesus' way. And "love your enemies" has never again regained its earlier place as the most quoted saying of Jesus.

Also, the church, the "body of Christ" in a fragmented world, has again and again been split into competing denominational in-groups. These groups have been obsessed with "their kind of people" and their "rightness," over against other Christians and other groups whom they judge to be wrong—those on "the other side"—Catholics, Baptists, Episcopalians, Presbyterians, Pentecostals, atheists, agnostics, Muslims, Buddhists, et al. And so Jesus' urgent call to go over to "the other side" to love those "enemies" who are so different from ourselves has been ignored, to the world's great hurt and the dishonoring of the name of Jesus. God help us.

Where might our dangerous crossing—our "mission impossible"— take us, should we commit ourselves to accept it? To the poor, surely. Jesus calls us to identify with them, to know and respect them as friends and equals, as sisters and brothers in the human struggle—the way he knew and loved them. That can be stormy, because the problems of our relating to the poorest members of our society are compounded by hundreds of years of racial and economic injustice, and by cultural differences and misunderstanding, along with our fears of the unfamiliar.

Of course there are other stormy gulfs to be crossed. Like the raging sea of alienation and misunderstanding and prejudice that separates gay and lesbian brothers and sisters from the heterosexual majority. Or the stormy gulf of injustice and discrimination that still separates women from men after so many centuries of male domination. Or the widening gulf that separates the generations and people of different faiths or no faith at all in this changing world. I could go on.

It won't be easy going with Jesus to "the other side." When we forsake our comfort zones and go with him, stormy times will inevitably come. Like those original disciples, we will sometimes feel that Jesus has gone to sleep on us, and we too will want to cry out, "Teacher, don't you care that we are perishing?"

Two of my good friends in ministry, African American Baptists, recently tried to lead their conventional, well-respected congregation into ministry with homeless people, with laborers who were struggling for a living wage and decent working conditions, and with young people in their neighborhood who were alienated from the church, dropping out of school, getting into drugs, and well on their way to big trouble: prison and, very likely, early graves. A vocal minority of staunch members of their congregation who couldn't see the wisdom of such dangerous crossings rose up and blocked renewal of the two pastors' calls. One night when all this was brewing, the senior pastor shook his head and said he felt like praying, "Lord, don't you care? Can't you see that we're going down?" He sounded as though he had this story in mind that night.

This familiar story in Mark carries a painfully relevant message. It leaves us with no pious illusions about the difficulty of the tasks to which Jesus calls us. The good news here is not that our journey of faith will be safe, easy, and successful, but that he whose saving power is greater than all the storms of life will always hear our cries and will never fail or forsake us. As the old hymn says, "The winds and waves still know the voice of him who ruled them when he dwelled below."

A word of personal testimony. Through the years since Jesus first hooked me with his "Follow me!" he has led and prodded and pushed me to cross over to "the other side." I know that it has deepened my faith, broadened my compassion, and enriched my life. In fact, when I retired from my last pastorate at the end of 1993, I entered into a ministry of helping people learn to work with those on "the other side" as equals who share a common responsibility for the integrity of our community.

This work is centered in an old house and a small church building in downtown Greensboro near the railroad tracks, where the world of stock brokers, bankers, and other professionals intersects with the lives of crack addicts, the homeless, and other poor people. We call our place the Beloved Community Center and use it to bring together representatives of these alienated worlds to meet one another on common ground, where they can begin to know one another as equals beloved by God. Here people are encouraged to open their minds and hearts to one another, to struggle with the strangeness of each other's views and experience, and to support one another in activities that will help Greensboro become a more just and loving community.

In the summer of 1995, some union workers, mostly black, from Greensboro's huge Kmart Distribution Center, came to their pastors and asked for help in improving their working conditions. They had been struggling for a union contract with that giant corporation for months and were getting nowhere. The ministers wanted to help them. They also saw this as a community struggle that could focus the city's attention on the need for decent wages and working conditions for all workers. So these pastors joined with the workers in a boycott of Kmart stores, beginning the day after Thanksgiving.

When the workers decided that direct action was necessary to get the company's attention, the ministers, in an effort to guarantee that the witness would remain nonviolent, offered to be the ones to act. They were subsequently arrested for praying together too close to the entrance of Greensboro's Super Kmart store and refusing to leave when told to do so. The week before these planned arrests, the pastors had asked us at the Beloved Community Center to host some meetings between them and some of Greensboro's business and professional leaders, whose understanding they wanted and needed as they entered into this dangerous public phase of the workers' struggle.

We at the Beloved Community Center were happy to help and gathered some community leaders who were willing to risk "crossing over to the other side" in conversations with the pastors and their labor allies. The group that met included a half dozen African American pastors, union workers (black and white), a former mayor of the city, the immediate past chair of the Chamber of Commerce, a couple of CEOs of small businesses, a couple of longtime community activists, a couple of white pastors, and a few others, some wealthy and some poor.

Through our weekly gatherings, we learned a great deal and truly changed one another by our "crossing over to the other side," both in those conversations and in our subsequent actions together. We also believe we played a significant part in influencing the Kmart company to agree to a union contract, which it did in July of 1996. And we are reasonably sure that we helped to raise the community's level of understanding and conversation about fundamental economic and spiritual issues in Greensboro.

The whole thing got scary at times. And there was reason to be scared, because we knew there was no telling what might happen next. But we were acting in the spirit of Jesus, nonviolently, in the interest of the beloved community—or, to use Jesus' words, the kingdom of God. All in all, it was a splendid, life-giving experience of "crossing over to the other side."

So, in Jesus' spirit, I invite you: "Let's cross over to the other side." Confidently, and often. And if I can help you, call on me.

ENDNOTES

1. Myers, *Binding the Strong Man*, 39.

5

Jesus' Tough Love

Mark 10:17–31

I RECENTLY READ A sermon from a colleague that contained these questions: "When was the last time someone from the church asked you how much money you make? Or what stocks you own? Or how much money you give to the church?" When I read those, I thought, that kind of meddling is usually not much appreciated by us Presbyterians. We don't talk to one another much about our money or our giving. At least we don't usually get that specific about it.

Many other denominational groups stress tithing their income for God's work and hold one another accountable for doing that, but we Presbyterians don't. Unless things have changed drastically since I retired from the pastorate, as a denomination we give something like two to three percent of our income to the church. We just don't like the church pressing us about our use of money.

In the sermon from the colleague, he suggested that for Presbyterians, *confidentiality* is the single most important noun connected with our giving. "It would be easy to conclude," he preached, "that this doctrine [of confidentiality] is more important than the doctrine of the resurrection [if you judge] by the way people get animated about who should see the pledge records."

So why *do* we have such difficulty talking about our relationship to our money? We talk about it plenty in other settings: discussing our business transactions, or complaining about taxes and the escalating cost of living. But we don't talk specifically about our income and our savings and investments in relation to our Christian commitment and our Christian responsibility for the way we use all of our resources.

As I think back on my ministry, I don't remember much talk in church about maintaining a faithful balance between what we were spending on our own comfortable lifestyles and what we were investing in Jesus' radical work of empowerment and healing among those trapped at the margins and in the hell holes of our society. So again I ask: Why can't we level with one another about our money, which is such an enormously important measure of human worth and human accomplishment in the eyes of our society, and so useful, if used wisely, in relieving human misery? Why does straight talk about these vital matters cause the saints in Presbyterian pews to cut their eyes around at one another as if to say, "Uh oh! Now he's quit preachin' and gone to meddlin'!"

Well, I aim to do some meddlin' here. And I'm doing it on good authority. The very least you could say about Jesus' conversation with the man in our Gospel reading is that Jesus was meddling in this wealthy brother's personal business. As Jesus and his disciples were setting out for Jerusalem, a man, who we later learn was a wealthy landowner, ran up to Jesus, knelt before him, and asked, "Good teacher, what must I do to inherit eternal life?"

Here was a man of property, a wealthy seeker, running up and falling on his knees before this itinerant teacher/prophet and honoring him with the greeting, "Good teacher," followed by a serious spiritual inquiry. That would have been startling, but it was not as surprising as Jesus' answer. What the man intended as a compliment and a show of deference calculated to win Jesus' favor is quickly brushed aside by Jesus' challenging response: "Why do you call me good? No one is good but God alone. You know the commandments: 'Do not kill, do not commit adultery, do not steal, do not bear false witness, do not defraud, honor your father and mother'" (Mark 10:18–19).

"Do not defraud"? That's not one of the Ten Commandments. Is Jesus confused here? Surely he knows the "10 C's"! I'll come back to that in a moment.

Some individuals might have been done in by Jesus' heavy words, "No one is good but God . . . You know the commandments . . ." That's straight talk—what these days we would call a putdown. But this is a confident man of wealth, and he is not put down by Jesus' straight talk. Instead, he presses on without hesitation or further deference.

"Teacher," he says, "all these [commandments] I have observed from my youth." *All* of them, brother? *Really?* I can't help but wonder. This young fellow is nothing if not confident of his uprightness. But then we read: "Jesus, looking at him, loved him, and said to him, 'You lack one thing; go, sell what you own, and give the money to the poor, and you will have treasure in heaven; and come, follow me.'"

If Jesus' initial response was tough, here's one that's super tough! It's one of the best instances in the gospels of what I call Jesus' "tough love." We ordinary human beings often use our love for a friend as an excuse for refusing to speak the plain truth to that friend concerning his/her destructive behavior. Not so with our friend Jesus, who loves us with a tough love. A revealing, challenging, transforming love. A terrifying love that refuses to equivocate but goes straight to the heart of our soul sickness.

Thanks be to God for such honest, terrifying love. Teachers and theologians and preachers have run end runs around the hard words of Jesus in this story for 2,000 years now. But here those words stand, to challenge us at the heart of our soul sickness amidst a society of unparalleled power and affluence—a society that practically worships at the altar of money and all the stuff that money can buy.

At Jesus' tough words of love, this confident brother's face fell. Shocked, he "went away, grieving, for he had many possessions." This is the only instance in the gospels where a person flatly rejects Jesus' call to discipleship. And why? Because he was wealthy, and Jesus insisted on liberating him from the terrible power of the possessions that were possessing him.

To help us understand our wealthy brother and ourselves better, let's go back to the command that Jesus slipped into his catalogue of the law: "Do not defraud." The economic system of Jesus' time defrauded the poor. Among the Jewish population, there were a few wealthy families, who owned most of the land, alongside many poor who were struggling for survival. Peasants on tiny farms were being crushed by ruinous taxes imposed by their own Jewish leaders and by Roman occupation forces.

At the same time, the wealthy few, who had inherited substantial ancestral estates, added to their wealth by serving as bankers for the peasants who, like the poor in this country today, were going under in increasing numbers. Many were already landless day laborers or slaves on the large estates of landowners like the man in this story. Others, who still retained small holdings, were constantly at the mercy of conflicts and natural calamities that wiped out their crops and made it necessary to borrow from the wealthy in order to stay afloat. With further disasters, they would lose their lands, which they had put up as collateral for the loans. In this way, owners of large estates worked the system to enlarge their holdings, and then took care to pass on their properties to their heirs—at the expense of the impoverished masses.

All this is the background of the man's confident question, "What must I do to *inherit* eternal life?" He had no doubt inherited his wealth and wanted Jesus to help him work the religious inheritance system for the ultimate prize: eternal life. Jesus, though, wasn't about to be a party to this man's game, or his sense of entitlement within a terribly unjust situation. He understood that the man's wealth was his prison—blocking his way to the new possibility that Jesus was offering to the world: being part of a community of love and sharing where there were neither rich nor poor but where all had enough.

So Jesus loved him enough to level with him. Jesus let him see that all of his properties and all of his imagined uprightness were a barrier between him and the suffering poor around him, who were dying for lack of a fraction of the stuff he was clinging to as if it were God. The wealthy man assumed that he could cut some deal with this "good teacher" that would allow him to keep his stuff, or at least parlay it into a more lasting inheritance of eternal life.

But this Teacher of ours is not into deals. And so he had to watch this brother, whom he loved, walk away grief-stricken. Then Jesus turned to his astonished disciples and said, "How hard it will be for those who have riches to enter the kingdom of God"—God's community of boundless love and sharing, where there are no rich and no poor; and where greatness is measured by one's service to all. As the disciples' amazement grew, Jesus continued, "Children, how hard it is to enter the kingdom of God. It is easier for a camel to go through the eye of a needle than for a rich man to enter the kingdom of God."

"Then who can be saved?" they cried.

He looked at them as he had looked at the rich brother and said, "For mortals it is impossible, but not for God; for God all things are possible."

And that's the truth—thanks be to God!

I don't know a Bible passage more relevant to our time and situation than this one. As I see it, most of us Americans, and certainly we relatively comfortable Presbyterians who don't like folks meddlin' in how we use our money, are prisoners. We are in voluntary servitude to the ruling powers of our society and their incessant urgings to consume and accumulate more and more stuff; to outdo our neighbors in consuming and accumulating, and in protecting and enlarging and passing on any wealth we have to our loved ones—regardless of what our lifestyle costs poor and desperate neighbors at home and abroad.

The powerful interests who would control us relentlessly urge us to find pleasure and contentment and the meaning of our lives in this self-centered quest for more: more money, more power, more status, a greater sense of entitlement to all that we have, and to the *rightness* of our having it. Through their marketing and spin, the ruling powers in our society tell us who we are, and who our enemies are, and what we are to fear and love and value and believe about our own rightness as we submit to their benevolent (?) rule.

This is a primary form of our society's tragic "slavery to sin," as the Apostle Paul would style it. And so we don't want to talk about the wealth we have, and how we use it, and how it blocks our faith in Jesus—that radical lover of the poor and the outcast and all the rest of us lonely victims of the greedy powers that be. Jesus, who loves us with his terrifyingly honest love.

Like our brother in this story, we are heirs of wealth taken fraudulently from the poor: from the natives of this land, from the African slaves and other people who worked it, and later from the children and immigrants who have toiled in mines and sweatshops and fields—all victims of greed and injustice, to whom the rest of us owe an incalculable debt. The great obstacle to our liberation from this condition of addiction to our society's ill-gotten plunder is the despairing fear that we can't change, because we are dependent upon what is wrong. That's the "addict's excuse," and it won't do.

As I see it, Jesus sees and understands this embarrassing addiction of ours, as he understood that rich brother's addiction so long ago. And he loves us with his tough love, and longs for us to break free and live. But one thing we must do, like the man in the story, and like the addicted brothers and sisters in our twelve-step recovery programs: Trusting in a Power greater than our own (God's love), we must break with our addiction and make our list of all those we have harmed in supporting it. And then we must undertake the long, liberating journey of making amends to them all, as we follow Jesus with grateful, burning hearts, clinging to his generous promise of forgiveness and transformed lives for all—even all of us rich and addicted folk.

Here are the words of that abundant promise: "Truly I say to you, there is no one who has left house or brothers or sisters or mother or father or children or lands for my sake and for the gospel, who will not receive a hundredfold now in this time, houses and brothers and sisters and mothers and children and lands, with persecutions, and in the age to come eternal life" (Mark 10:29–30).

That "with persecutions" is a powerful insertion that calls for another sermon in the near future. And you shall have it. I promise.

6

A Crooked Manager?

Luke 16:1–9

THE STORY OF THE "dishonest steward" is surely one of the most difficult of Jesus' parables. It has puzzled generations of Christian teachers and preachers. The proverbial sayings about wealth that follow in Luke's text increase the perplexity, coming across as three or four different efforts to sum up the meaning of the parable:

> Whoever is faithful in a very little is faithful also in much; and whoever is dishonest in a very little is dishonest also in much. If then you have not been faithful with the dishonest wealth, who will entrust to you the true riches? And if you have not been faithful with that which belongs to another, who will give you what is your own? No slave can serve two masters; for a slave will either hate the one and love the other, or be devoted to the one and despise the other. You cannot serve God and wealth. (Luke16:10–13)

Puzzling, no? There's a lot of truth in these words, but they don't help us much in getting to the point of the strangest of Jesus' parables. To me, this repetitious collection of sayings sounds like Luke's—or some other early Christian teacher's—effort to make sure that his readers wouldn't take the parable to mean that Jesus condoned the deceit of the parable's main character—the "dishonest steward," as he is usually characterized.

Consider the ethical problems presented by the parable's main character. This steward is the manager of a wealthy man's estate. In the course of this brief story, we learn about this fellow:

- First, that he has been accused of wasting his master's goods;
- Second, that he is soft: "I'm too weak to dig," he confesses;

36

- Third, he is also proud: ". . . and I'm ashamed to beg," he says;

- Fourth, he is willing to be a sponger: he wants other people to solve his personal unemployment problem by taking him into their homes after he is fired;

- Fifth, he appears quite self-centered: from his first words, "What shall I do?" to the end of the story, he shows little regard either for his employer's interests or for the people he is setting up to bail him out (he has *them* write the fraudulent, reduced IOUs);

- And finally, he corrupts others: by seducing his master's debtors into cutting their bills, he makes them accomplices in his survival scheme and sets them up to be blackmailed by him later if he should wish to do so.

This steward comes across as an incompetent, weak, proud sponger who, out of self-interest, corrupts others. To call him "dishonest" is, as commentator James Breech observed, "to call attention to his least un-attractive quality."[1] So one problem with the parable is its questionable leading character.

Even more troubling is the fact that, after learning of this fellow's scheme for survival without a job, we read that "his master *commended* the dishonest manager because he had acted shrewdly." Amazing! But then it continues, "for the children of this age are more shrewd in dealing with their own generation than are the children of light" (Luke 16:8).

The question this statement brings to my mind is, who is this master who commended such a character? His wealthy employer, whom he had just bilked out of the first-century equivalent of thousands of dollars? The more likely answer, I think, is Jesus, who is telling this story. For the words that immediately follow are clearly his: "And I tell you, make friends for yourselves by means of dishonest wealth so that when it is gone, they may welcome you into the eternal homes." (Luke 16:9). That, I believe, is the point of the story—spelled out by Jesus at the end of it. It's a teaching about the intended use of wealth.

And yet . . . if these *are* Jesus' words, what are we to make of his commendation of this rascal for his shrewd behavior? Interestingly, the Roman emperor Julian the Apostate, who tried to take the "Christian" Roman Empire back to its earlier paganism, defended his "apostasy" from Christianity by citing this story. He declared that a man who would tell such a story couldn't be "divine"!

I believe Jesus' words of commendation here confront us with a double challenge. First, they challenge our tendency to sanitize Jesus in ways that rob him of his humanity and his radicalism. The very presence of this unsavory, worldly story in Luke's gospel implies that Jesus was not as fastidious in his teaching as many of us followers have tended to imagine. He obviously thought that his followers could learn from the shrewd rascal in this real-life story.

In fact, Jesus often depicted the behavior of real rascals in his stories. The "prodigal son" comes to mind as a prime example. That kid was what would be called a punk in today's street jargon. By our much sentimentalizing of the boy, we have inadvertently sanitized him. But the prodigal, like the steward here, was not a consistently admirable character at all. He was simply a headstrong, immature young man who—after he had blown his inheritance—finally exercised the good sense to go home, where he knew he was loved and hoped he would be received.

My point is that Jesus paid attention to human beings of all sorts, learned from them, and presented them in his stories without sanitizing or making moralistic value judgments about them. Such was the measure of his compassion—his love for *all*. There was no pious "spin" in Jesus' reporting. He saw life with great clarity, warts and all. And, as old sports commentator Howard Cosell used to say, he told it "like it is." If this makes Jesus less "holy" than we would like for him to be, that's *our* problem.

Second, Jesus' words of commendation to the steward confront our tendency to soften and diminish his radical challenge to our half-hearted discipleship, and our inclination to condemn the clever rascals of this world—rather than giving them the respect they are due and learning from them. In his remark about the "children of this age" being more shrewd than the "children of light," Jesus is making the point that irreligious folk whose hopes are limited to this world often tend to be sharper and more seriously committed to pursuing life as they understand it than we who claim to live by the light and Spirit of God. A heavy indictment, for sure; but who can deny the truth in it?

The most demanding educational experience to which I was exposed as a young person was the U.S. Navy's flight training program. It kept me stretching, straining, and scrambling each step along the way, wondering whether I could pass that day's test. But I never was challenged like that by Sunday school—or by any other program of any of the churches in which

I participated as a young person. I wasn't even challenged at that level by my courses at Davidson College or Union Theological Seminary.

So why weren't the teaching efforts of church, college, and seminary as challenging and disturbing as the Navy's flight training? Is it because learning to be an effective naval aviator and an efficient killer for the U.S. government is more important than preparing to be a courageous, deeply committed follower of Jesus? I think not. Then is it because of the strange tendency of us Christian "children of light" to take a lackadaisical attitude toward the life-transforming gifts that God offers us in Jesus Christ? I suspect so.

It is true that growing numbers of "the children of this age" who profess no faith in God nevertheless give their passionate best to life as they understand it. I'm talking about hard-driving business people, effective politicians, diligent professionals and artists, winning coaches and athletes, and a host of others who live and compete passionately, who call forth the best in their associates, and who think furiously about the transient and often trivial enterprises to which they give their lives and energies.

But what of us "children of light"? We followers of Jesus revere the Bible, but too few of us take the trouble required to understand and live by its challenging message. We believe in prayer but, God forgive us, are too rushed to get around to a seriously disciplined prayer life. We suspect Jesus wants us to get out of our comfort zones and into the highways and the hassles of those who are being crushed by the terrible injustices and conflicts of our time. But, God forgive us, we lack precisely the urgency of purpose and focus and courage for decisive action that the questionable character in Jesus' parable displayed. Jesus' challenge to us is to look at the "worldly winners" and be reminded by them to pursue the eternally significant, world-changing work of God's beloved community at least as seriously as they (and we) pursue transient concerns.

But now, to the main point of the parable, which caused the gospel writer to place this story at the beginning of a chapter largely devoted to Jesus' teaching about the proper use of wealth. "I tell you," said Jesus, "make friends of dishonest wealth so that when it is gone, they may welcome you into the eternal homes." This crooked manager used his master's wealth *to make friends*. He obviously intended to cash in on his generous reduction of the debts of these friends when his generosity got him in trouble with the boss.

But now consider this: he may well have been doing the same sort of thing for his employer's impoverished debtors all along—doing it in good conscience to subvert an unjust system. And when his boss discovered it, that's why he called this much too generous steward to account for his stewardship. Maybe the steward had been "making friends" with his master's money all along, as a nonviolent protest against his wealthy employer's fleecing of poor debtors. It could have been this fellow's practice of "redistributive justice" that had gotten him into trouble in the first place.

I can imagine also that Jesus heard of this steward's story and proceeded to use it to teach his followers what money is ultimately good for: making friends. It's for reaching out to victims of an unjust world and using the means at one's disposal to help them. That certainly is the way Jesus would have us use our resources.

"Give to everyone who begs from you," he commanded (Matthew 5:42; Luke 6:30). And to his host at table on one occasion, he said, "When you give a luncheon or a dinner, do not invite your friends or your brothers or your relatives or rich neighbors, in case they may invite you in return, and you would be repaid. But when you give a banquet, invite the poor, the crippled, the lame, and the blind. And you will be blessed, because they cannot repay you, for you will be repaid at the resurrection of the righteous" (Luke 14:12–14).

In other words, use your wealth to befriend those whom God hurts for and wants befriended. Use your resources to bring food where there's hunger, to bring health where there's illness, to bring hope and reconciliation where there's despair and alienation: to establish real justice and peace in the land. Use your money to make friends. Subvert the human tendency to use it to put down rivals and competitors, to make oneself richer and others poorer, and so to make conflict inevitable and community impossible.

If there is any truth to the Christian faith and its hope of resurrection to eternal life, then eternal life has to do not with accumulation of money and wealth, but with friends. It has to do with those relationships with God and with others that are the true treasure of this world—the treasure that we hope will be renewed and continued and enjoyed for all eternity.

Money, if it's to fulfill its intended function in the eternal purposes of God, must be *transformed here and now into love*—translated into caring for those for whom God wants abundant life and community, not poverty and alienation. The preparation that we all need for eternal life is not fat bank accounts and fatter investment portfolios. Rather, we need the day by day enlargement of our hearts and souls that comes from generously sharing our lives and our goods with those who need what has been entrusted to us, which is ours to give.

There is much to be learned from this (at first glance) unsavory little story of Jesus. First, Jesus loved and learned gladly from those whom the righteous would have dismissed as rascals, and he would free us all from the sort of fearful conformity that would keep us from loving and learning from all sorts, as he did. Second, Jesus calls those of us who have seen the light of the gospel ("the children of light") to live lives that are at least as focused and passionately committed as the lives of the worldly wise winners celebrated by our culture. And third, Jesus saw in the behavior of the "crooked" steward a testimony to what money is really for: making friends for God and for the sake of the happiness of God's beloved and loving community, now and for all eternity.

Ched Myers, a good friend and superlative biblical scholar and liberation theologian, has suggested that I have overdone the "crookedness" and self-centeredness of the steward in the parable. He reminded me that wealthy landowners like the master in this story regularly reduced the peasants to whom they loaned money for farming to a form of landless slavery. This they did by charging exorbitant interest on such loans. And then, when droughts or storms came, and crops failed, and the peasants couldn't pay, they took the peasants' tiny parcels of land, adding these to their great estates and reducing the former owners to debt slavery, making them hired laborers on the land they had once owned.

The steward in this parable was evidently a manager of such an estate. We can imagine that the basis for the charges brought against him for "wasting" his master's property were related to his doing a compassionate version of the very thing he did to secure his own future: he was subverting an unfair system by reducing the debtors' debts on occasion in order to enable them to pay up and retain their land. We can imagine, further, that others in the master's employ, or even some peasants who didn't get in on this compassionate subversion of the system, went and told the master what was happening. Hence the master's demand of an accounting from his estate manager.

But if that was what had been happening on this steward's watch, the peasants with whom he did business might even have had a warm spot in their hearts for the "generous" master who (as they would perceive it) allowed his steward to practice such compassionate generosity. And the years of that subversive manager's service for the master would have been the most peaceful in anyone's memory! So when the master heard about his manager's subversive generosity, called for the accounting, and learned of how his steward handled the crisis, he might well have commended the fellow for his shrewdness and smiled as he did so—becoming, along with the indebted peasants, an admiring friend of his subversive, "liberation theologian" of a manager who had brought a whole new spirit to the master's enterprise.

Speculation? Sure. But this is a story. The sort of realistic, yet surprising, story that Jesus loved to tell; from which his followers are free to discern many life-giving meanings and insights into their own situations. Whichever way you interpret it, the point remains: Use the filthy lucre that is the occasion of so much mischief in this greedy world to make friends. For love and friendship will last, long after money (and this world) are gone.

ENDNOTES

1. Breech, *The Silence of Jesus*, 109.

7

Community building Economics

Matthew 20:1–15 & Exodus 16:2–20

W HY WOULD ANYONE PREACH a sermon about community-building economics? That's a fair question, since economics as practiced these days seems to be just about the least religious subject, and least productive of community, that one might choose. Also, it is one that makes us Presbyterians, and I'm guessing others, pretty uncomfortable in the context of worship. In my experience, it makes congregations squirm even more than talk about sex, which is difficult enough to address in church.

But I'm going to talk about economics. Not free-market capitalism, the economic system that is rapidly covering the globe, making the rich richer and the poor poorer. Instead, I'm going to talk about what I have called community-building economics, because I believe that it is the practice that is consistent with God's will. I'm talking about the kind of economic perspective that Jesus had in mind when he taught his disciples to pray, "Your kingdom come, your will be done *on earth*"; and "Give us this day *our daily bread*"; and "Forgive us *our debts* as we forgive *our debtors.*" And when he declared, "You cannot serve God and *wealth.*"

I mean the kind of economics Jesus had in mind the day he told his astonished dinner host and the other guests around the table to invite the outcasts, who cannot repay their generosity, when they held a banquet. I mean the generous, humane kind of economic activity that creates trust and mutual respect among a variety of neighbors, rather than setting them against one another in perpetual competition for more stuff.

Matthew's parable is a story about what we call labor-management relations. In it we are told that an employer goes out very early in the morning to the local labor pool—like the one on South Eugene Street across from Greensboro Urban Ministry and others like it all across this country—where people hang around, hoping for work. This vineyard owner goes out at six o'clock in the morning to hire some day laborers. He agrees with a group of the workers there to pay them the normal daily wage, probably a bare living wage, for their labors. And then he sends them to work in his vineyard.

All of this is consistent with what we know of employment practices in Jesus' time. That's the way Jesus' parables and most of his teachings work: they are stories from real life—not otherworldly talk, but stories based on the way things are. That has always been their power: they speak to ordinary people about the everyday issues of our life experience.

But the parables also have a deeper, disturbing quality. They are real-life stories with an unexpected twist that catches us off guard and hooks us into considering the possibilities of life as God intends it to be; the possibilities of an alternative world of love and community beyond our fondest dreams. It was that kind of beloved and loving community that Jesus had in view when he spoke of the kingdom of God.

In this parable, Jesus begins to set his hook right at the beginning. He tells us that this employer comes back to the labor pool at nine o'clock. He sees others standing there idle, and tells them, "You also go into the vineyard and I will pay you whatever is right." And so they go. But that's not all. He comes back again at noon, and again at three o'clock in the afternoon, and does the same thing.

Strangest of all, the vineyard owner comes back at five o'clock, an hour before quitting time. He finds others standing around and says to them, "Why are you standing here idle all day?" They answer, "Because no one has hired us." So he says, "You also go into the vineyard." And without any specific agreement about the pay, they go—apparently trusting this strange fellow who can't stand seeing folks hanging around without work.

All of this is odd, but by no means as strange as the next development. The employer calls his foreman at the end of the day and instructs him to pay all the workers the full day's wage. Not only that, he tells him to pay those who were employed at five o'clock in the afternoon first!

The foreman does as he's told, first paying a full day's wage to those hired at the end of the day. Well, you can imagine how this computed in the minds of the ones hired earlier—especially for those who had worked since six o'clock that morning. If the boss was paying a full day's wage for one hour's work, the others stood to get three times, or six, or nine, or even twelve times that much! But each group in turn gets exactly the same pay: the customary wage that the first set of workers had originally agreed to.

Understandably, the first group, the six a.m. fellows, are really hacked. "These last worked only one hour, and you have made them equal to us who have borne the burden of the day and the scorching heat," they complain. Let's be honest here, wouldn't *you* complain—or at least feel like complaining—if you were in their shoes? I'm pretty sure I would. So what are we to make of this employer's odd behavior?

Traditionally, Bible interpreters have said something like this: This is not really a story about economics at all. It's a story about the grace of God, and how God is equally gracious toward all believers—whether they come on board the salvation train early or late. It's about the love of God, and there's no such thing as a twelfth part of the love of God (the "fair share" due the five o'clock people). Each of us workers in God's vineyard gets a full share, thank God. And those who have known God's love a long time should never complain about the brothers and sisters who almost missed knowing it.

Well, you can interpret the parable that way. Great teachers of mine, whom I love and respect, do interpret it that way, and certainly I would never quarrel with the beautiful message of grace that they find in it. That's the way I preached and taught it myself, for years. But recently I've begun to wonder whether that's all that Jesus had in mind when he told the story.

In the first place, if the employer symbolizes God in the story, it shows God in a right bad light—especially if you look at it from the workers' point of view. This employer surely knew how the all-day workers were likely to feel when the foreman paid the one-hour people the same wage as theirs. Not only did it make those who worked only an hour "equal" to these who worked all day in the scorching heat. In a sense it devalued the labor of the workers hired first, as though they were worth only a twelfth as much per hour as the latecomers.

It's as though this employer needs a tax deduction. He's feeling "charitable" and using his wealth in an ostentatious way that makes him feel good about himself—without ever realizing that he's making all the workers except the last group feel devalued. Then, when they complain, he says, rather pompously, "Friend, I'm doing you no wrong. Didn't you agree with me for the usual daily wage? Now take your money and go. I choose to give to these last folks the same as I gave to you. Am I not allowed to do what I choose with my own money? Are you envious because I'm generous?"

Now put yourself in the position of today's farm workers, and imagine your employer, an agribusiness tycoon, making that speech at you when you complain about his hiring temporaries and paying them the same as he pays you who've been with the company thirty years. That will give you a feel for why liberation theologians—people who interpret the Bible from the perspective of the struggling, marginal workers of this world—don't like that traditional interpretation that my teachers offered me and that I preached for many years. It makes a gracious, godlike hero of this employer, who seems less than godlike when seen through the eyes of most of his workers.

So what are we to make of this story? Is it a parable of the extraordinary grace of God, who deals with all of us not in proportion to what we deserve, but in terms of our need for employment in the work of the kingdom, and for a full portion of God's love to sustain us in it? Or is it a story exposing the flaw in insensitive "charity"—the use of wealth and position to inflate one's own sense of righteousness and generosity without regard for what it does to the sense of self-worth and accomplishment of the poor, thereby creating among them the sort of envy and anger that keeps them divided against one another and subservient to people like this man? Or . . . could Jesus have intended his story to reveal both God's grace and the way it is often violated in our efforts to do good? I think Jesus probably intended his story to carry both of these messages.

I think we find the inspiration for this parable in the Old Testament, which we know as Jesus' Bible. It's found especially in the story of the manna by which God fed the Israelites in the wilderness when they were fleeing slavery in Egypt. As slaves under the control of that great empire, the children of Israel had had food to eat. Nothing great, most likely, but food. Having been liberated under Moses' leadership, they find themselves in the desert—hungry. So they complain that this new freedom of theirs is too tough: "If only we had died by the hand of the Lord in the land of Egypt, when we sat by those kettles of stew and ate our fill of bread; now you have brought us out into this wilderness to kill us all by starvation."

And how does God respond to their complaint? Through Moses, God promises to "rain bread down from heaven" for them. Now we can't know from this distance exactly how that worked, or just how literally the writer of the story wanted us readers to take it. But a couple of crucial items are very clear from this story:

First, Moses is instructed to tell every family to gather *only enough* of this "bread from heaven" for their own family's needs. And this they did, "some gathering more, some gathering less." Then we read: "But when they measured it . . . those who had gathered much had nothing over, and those who gathered little had no shortage."

In God's economy, there's no place for some having too much and others having too little, because God provides plenty for everyone. That's the first principle of "community economics"—business practices by which God's will is done on earth. It goes all the way back to Israel's beginnings.

This principle is badly violated by our present global economy. According to a 1992 United Nations report, "the wealthiest 20 percent of the world's population receives almost 83 percent of the world's income, while the poorest 20 percent receive less than 2 percent." It's violated also by our own nation's economy, where in 1998 the average worker made "$7.39 per hour and the average CEO $1,566.68 per hour—212 times more."[1] Since then, the disparity has grown dramatically and continues to widen.

The workers in Jesus' parable were to be like the early Israelite families: each laborer, who surely needed a living wage for himself and his family, received it, just as each hungry family in the wilderness received bread according to their need. The strange employer in Jesus' parable was carrying out the first principle of Israel's liberation economics: God's economics of enough for everyone.

We see this principle exemplified not only here but often in Jesus' ministry. In the feeding of the five thousand, for example. Or his instruction to invite the poor and excluded to our dinners rather than using all our precious resources in exchanging social obligations with family and friends. Or his charge to a wealthy would-be disciple to sell his property, give the proceeds to the poor, and come and follow him. Many more examples follow in the addendum at the end of this reflection.

The point is that Jesus read his Bible, embraced God's community-building economic practice of enough for everyone (as set forth in the Exodus story), and made it the model for the employer's odd but gracious treatment of his laborers in this parable. Jesus wanted his hearers to be reminded by this story of the way goods are to be shared and workers paid in God's beloved community: a wage that is "right." And that is what the employer promises his workers in Jesus' story. But I suspect that Jesus also wanted to alert those with wealth to the dangers of self-righteous "charity"—the sort of ostentatious generosity that is self-congratulatory and demeaning to the poor who are its recipients.

This is a story about life as it can and should be, by the grace of God. But it's also a story of how our generosity can be corrupted by our need to set ourselves up as superior to others. The generous employer, insofar as he is generous, is very like God, in that he is reflecting the sort of attitude toward "bread"—the economic side of life—that Israelites had been called to embody ever since their liberation from economic slavery themselves. Insofar as his display of generosity is self-serving and more or less demeaning to the workers hired earlier than the ones who worked only the last hour of the day, he is very like the self-serving wealthy who paraded their pious generosity in the market places in Jesus' time: the folk who come under rather heavy critical scrutiny in his Sermon on the Mount (See Matthew 6:1–4).

As for the workers in the parable, they are like all of us, who need an opportunity to be engaged in worthwhile, productive work, rather than standing around idle and devalued by society—like the people, many of them homeless, who stand around daily on South Eugene Street hoping for a day's work. The employment of such folk at a wage far greater than they could have expected is consistent with Jesus' generous treatment of the excluded and devalued whom he welcomed to a full share in God's beloved community. That's the good news in this story. The sad part of it is the self-congratulatory speech of the generous owner of the vineyard and the envious, self-serving complaint of the other workers when they saw those hired last treated so generously.

So this parable serves as a mirror, I think, in which we can catch a glimpse of how community economics, based on trust in a bountiful God and generous sharing that cares for the needs of all, might be acted out among us. But it also mirrors flaws in all of us—rich and poor, employers and employees, benefactors and those benefited—flaws that make economic justice a challenge to us all. In the end, this story is a call to repentance and to action in order to make our own and our society's economic practices and attitudes reflect the generosity of God: God's community-building economics. This strangely beautiful and troubling parable is a challenge to employers and employees alike to test their relationships by their bountiful Creator's will that all should enjoy earth's bounty in a spirit of beloved community.

ADDENDUM: JESUS' STRANGE ATTITUDE TOWARD WEALTH

(Jesus vs. Common Sense)

1. **Common Sense**: We should always get a good return on our investments (the cost-benefit principle)

   Jesus: *When you give a dinner or a banquet, do not invite your friends or your brothers or your relatives or rich neighbors, in case they may invite you in return and you be repaid. But when you give a banquet, invite the poor, the crippled, the lame, and the blind. And you will be blessed, because they cannot repay you, for you will be repaid at the resurrection of the righteous* (Luke 14:12–13).

2. **Common Sense**: The rich, the well fed, the fun-loving people of this world are the ones who are happy and blessed.

   Jesus: *Blessed are you poor, for yours is the kingdom of God. Blessed are you who hunger now, for you shall be satisfied. Blessed are you that weep now, for you shall laugh* (Luke 6:20–21).

3. **Common Sense**: You can serve God while pursuing wealth as the source of your security.

   Jesus: *No one can serve two masters; for a slave will either hate the one and love the other, or be devoted to the one and despise the other. You cannot serve God and wealth* (Matthew 6:24).

4. **Common Sense**: You can cling to your wealth and still follow Jesus.

   Jesus: *Whoever of you does not renounce all that he/she has cannot be my disciple* (Luke 14:33).

5. **Common Sense**: The more money you save, the more you will have.

   Jesus: *Give, and it will be given to you. A good measure, pressed down, shaken together, running over, will be put into your lap; for the measure you give will be the measure you get back* (Luke 6:38).

6. **Common Sense**: Don't give to beggars or lend to bad risks.

   Jesus: *Give to everyone who begs from you and do not refuse anyone who wants to borrow from you* (Matthew 5:42).

7. **Common Sense**: To carry out the Christian mission, we must have lots of money and spacious facilities at our disposal.

Jesus (to his missionaries): *Take no gold, or silver, or copper in your belts, no bag for your journey, or two tunics, or sandals, or a staff . . .* (Matthew 10:9).

8. **Common Sense**: The evidence that salvation has come to a person is a stable life, growing prosperity, and conscientious tithing.

Jesus: See the story of the widow's mite (Mark 12:41–44); Jesus' encounter with Zaccheus (Luke 19:1–10); the calling of the first disciples (Mark 1:16–20); and the rich man's question (Mark 10:17–30).

9. **Common Sense**: Plan and work and save toward the goal of financial security, and you will be freed to enjoy the good things of life.

Jesus (concerning anxiety over the physical necessities of life): *Your heavenly Father knows that you need all these things. But seek first the kingdom of God and his righteousness, and all these things will be given to you as well* (Matthew 6:32b-33). See also the parable of the rich fool (Luke 12:13–21) and the story of the rich man and Lazarus (Luke 16:19–31).

Conclusion: Common Sense (i.e., the popular wisdom of our affluent society) tells us: Wealth is to be desired, trusted, accumulated, and guarded as the source of our security and power in this competitive world.

But **Jesus** seems to believe that *God* is to be desired, trusted, loved, and served as the source of our security and power; and wealth is to be used, shared, given, and enjoyed in the service and care of the community, especially its poorest and neediest members.

ENDNOTES

1. Quoted by Ched Myers in *Sojourners*, May-June 1998, 25–26.

8

Jesus Speaks to the "Neighbor Problem"

Luke 10:25–37

I BELIEVE IT WAS George Orwell who said, "To see what is in front of one's nose needs a constant struggle." Regardless of who said it, it's not a bad motto for our present age of confusion and struggle for full inclusion of all our neighbors as equals. Certainly Jesus would agree that seeing is a constant struggle. "Do you still not perceive or understand?" he pleaded with his disciples. "Are your hearts hardened? Do you have eyes and fail to see?" (Mark 8:17–18)

Through this story from the Gospel of Luke, Jesus can help us in our constant struggle to see—truly *see*—what is in front of our noses. In it, a lawyer (what we would call a theologian) stands up to test Jesus one day. "What must I do to inherit eternal life?" he asks.

Jesus responds with his own questions: "What is written in the law? What do you read there?"

The man answers, "You shall love the Lord your God with all your heart, and with all your soul, and with all your strength, and with all your mind; and your neighbor as yourself."

"Right!" says Jesus. "Do this and you will live." Question answered. End of conversation.

But we theologians don't like short conversations that leave us feeling uncomfortable, so this brother presses the issue. "And who is my neighbor?" he asks, as though to say, "It's not as simple as you seem to think, Jesus."

Obviously this brother had a problem—not with the part about God, mind you. This was a religious man, and if religion is about anything, it is about the love of God. On that, religious people of all persuasions seem to agree. What bothered him—and bothers religious folk still—was the part about the neighbor who is to be loved as oneself. It's our troublesome neighbors who can make us forget about love, even forget about God.

Why? Let's face it, some neighbors just don't seem fit to be loved. I think, for example, of drug kingpins who seem to have no respect for the lives, young and old, that their cruel business destroys. Or consider the petty bullies of this world who intimidate their employees and abuse their own loved ones and neighbors, to say nothing of their competitors. Or think of those who have made international terrorism their weapon of choice in advancing their religious and political aims. Or closer to home, consider our own leaders who adopted a policy of preemptive war as a legitimate "defense" against those whom they identify as evil—and are willingly sacrificing the lives of our young people in pursuit of this policy. Are "neighbors" such as these to be loved as oneself?

To put it another way: Where do you draw the line between the neighbor who is to be loved as oneself and those in the world who certainly appear to require very different treatment? Don't we have to draw the line *somewhere*—or else be wiped out trying to do good to everybody and sympathize with everybody's problems?

Help with our struggle over where to draw the line is available to us in Luke's account of Jesus' parable of the Good Samaritan. It's a story that would have surprised and deeply offended his original hearers, but whose shock value has been largely lost through much retelling that has blunted its radical message.

The first surprise in this story is its setting. To show this religious teacher his neighbor, Jesus invites him to imagine himself far from the synagogue with its worship and its theological discussions. The action in Jesus' story takes place on the road from Jerusalem to Jericho—a wild, godforsaken place—dangerous, deserted, the haunt of desperate men. In this very non-religious setting, a Jew is traveling, perhaps a Jewish teacher of the law like Jesus' questioner, on pilgrimage to the temple in Jerusalem.

Suddenly the traveler is set upon by thieves, who not only rob him but strip him as well, then beat him, and leave him there to die. Surely the implication of the story's setting is that it's not in the safety of synagogue or temple, among like-minded friends, but out in the everyday world, with its dangers and violence and suffering, that Jesus is inviting his questioner to see the answer to the question about who is (and who is not) his neighbor.

Jesus would do the same for us, I believe. To show us our neighbor, he would invite us out of the safety and familiarity of our homes and sanctuaries and into the streets, to the places of danger and poverty and pain. Maybe to the poor neighborhoods where the drug trade is rampant, where violence is a continual threat and life is brutally hard and often tragically short. Jesus wants his hearers to identify with the dying victim in his parable, to imagine themselves in his place, helpless and in terrible need. From this unaccustomed perspective, Jesus would have us see with new eyes who the neighbor is that we are to love as ourselves.

Now the plot thickens. The first traveler to arrive on the gory scene is a priest, probably on his way to Jerusalem to serve in the temple (in our case, to "preach at his church up the street.") He sees the dying man (yourself, remember) in the ditch. As the victim, you think, "Praise the Lord! Here comes a man of God, sent to help me." But no. As soon as this passerby sees you lying there, he crosses the road and hurries by on the other side.

Why, you wonder. Why would he leave me here like this? But we can imagine why, can't we? FEAR! This passing preacher—excuse me, this priest—is probably thinking to himself, "The hoodlums who did this are probably still around here, looking for another victim, so let me get out of here while I can!"

More than that, in Jesus' world priests had to be ritually clean to serve in the temple, and contact with a dead body was the worst kind of defilement, according to the law. So trying to help a person who could die any minute was a risky job for a priest. It could disqualify him for his priestly duties.

In his fright, the priest may well have said a prayer for the victim and vowed to tell the Jerusalem authorities to look into the matter. But Jesus doesn't tell us why this man of God passed by. He leaves that for us to figure out from our own experience, for he knows that we all have our self-justifying reasons.

Next on the scene is a Levite, a layman with responsibilities around the temple—like a church custodian, or choir director, or even a deacon or elder. He too sees you lying there. When you see him, you feel a fresh surge of hope. But then he too crosses to the other side of the road and hurries by. Why? Jesus again declines to say. But we can well imagine that he too was scared—concerned to save his own skin and ensure that his wife wouldn't be a widow and his children orphans.

The point is that, twice over, Jesus pictures for us the failure of good and respectable people—religious leaders—to help this wounded man. They saw him, of course. But they saw him through eyes of fear, saw him as an unknown, saw him as a threat to their own safety and peace of mind. They recognized the victim as a signal to keep moving and stay out of the kind of trouble that had overtaken this poor fellow.

They represent the fear and inaction of decent religious people—the sort of fear of involvement that allows the victims of society's evils and injustices to continue suffering and dying at a terrible rate. I think it is fair to say Jesus wants us to see ourselves—our fears and our failures to help—in these passersby, just as he wants us to see our vulnerability and need in the beaten man.

But then comes the big surprise—the real shocker. A Samaritan comes down the road. Why a surprise? Because a Samaritan is not supposed to be on this road. This is Jewish territory. A Samaritan here is like the president of the NAACP at a rally of the Ku Klux Klan.

The Jews and Samaritans were bitter enemies—had been enemies for more than five hundred years when Jesus told this story. Their mutual hatred had been aggravated by some recent atrocities and was therefore especially intense at that time. So a Samaritan was about the least likely hero of a Jewish story that anyone in Jesus' audience would have imagined.

The Samaritan's role in this tale would have been not only totally unexpected but totally unacceptable. There would have been angry shuffling and murmurs of disapproval among Jesus' hearers (the equivalent of modern catcalls). But Jesus presses on—on to the biggest shocker of all.

The hated Samaritan sees the wounded man—really *sees* him. And he has compassion. That is, he feels for him, feels with him, feels his pain and his dangerous situation. For some reason he can't properly harden his heart against this dying Jew, his enemy.

He somehow sees past the threat to his own safety, of which there was plenty! After all, he was a traveler in enemy territory who could have expected no mercy from the robbers if they were still around, or from the earlier passersby, or even from the victim himself, if he had not been disabled. Seemingly oblivious to danger, the Samaritan simply sees another human being like himself, in trouble, near death, in need of help.

So he goes to the victim, eases his pain, treats his wounds, lifts him up on his own donkey, and takes him to the safety of an inn. There he nurses this enemy out of danger, then leaves money and instructions that will ensure the man's further care, and goes on his way.

This Samaritan may have been—no doubt was—afraid for his own life, which was certainly endangered by his actions. He may have hated the very sight of blood, may have had a wife and five children back in Samaria depending on him, waiting for him to come back home. He would almost certainly have been prejudiced against Jews; that went with being a Samaritan.

But Jesus tells us nothing of his thoughts or his fears, only of his compassion and his deeds. What he does in Jesus' story he does without fanfare, without a single overtly "religious" gesture. He does what he does simply for a victim suffering from human wickedness, a total stranger, a traditional enemy—but for all that, a fellow human being like himself.

At the end of this thoroughly offensive story, Jesus turns to his learned questioner and asks, "Which one of these proved neighbor to the man who fell among robbers?" Not, "Which one believed that he should love God with his whole heart and his neighbor as himself?" Not, "Which one went to synagogue regularly and studied the law?" Not, "Which one had the proper racial, religious, and social pedigree?"

The priest and Levite were believers and presumably had all the proper credentials. But Jesus asked which one *proved* a neighbor to the wounded man. That is, which one treated the wounded man as he himself would want to be treated?

"The one who showed mercy" answers the theologian—his eyes now open to seeing life through the eyes of a victim, even if he couldn't speak the hated name "Samaritan." Jesus then instructs him to go with what he has seen, and *do* it. And that's the end of the encounter as Luke tells it.

In the theologian's question, "Who is my neighbor?" is a hidden assumption—namely, that some people are *not* neighbors who are to be loved as oneself. In asking the question this way, he was thinking of himself as we are inclined to do, as being in the center of a circle of neighborly love. And he was trying to decide who should be admitted to his circle.

Whom do I let in, and whom had I better keep out of my "neighbor" circle? That was his question, as it is ours. Whom are we to admit to the full fellowship of the church, with all its privileges and responsibilities? Or to the club? Or to the family? Or to full citizenship? Or to my financial resources and my home? Who gets into the circle of love and neighborliness that I, and the others in my circle, control? These are the kinds of questions implied in the man's initial question.

So what does Jesus' answer do for this theologian? His offensive story wrests control from the questioner, yanks him out of the center of his familiar circle of loved ones and friends, and drops him into a ditch— bleeding, dying, helpless. Jesus lets the story ask and answer the questions: Whom would you admit to your circle of love under these circumstances? Whose love would you be willing to accept when you're all but done for and your friends are passing you by? Love and help from people you despise and would ordinarily exclude—would you accept that?

In spite of my prejudices, I would have to admit, "Yes, Lord, to save myself and my loved ones I would accept the compassion even of those I have looked down on and despised—even old ___ [Here you must fill in the names]. Yes, I would let even those people into my circle of love."

You see, this radical, offensive parable does not tell us how, exactly, to go about loving our troublesome neighbors; it simply offers us a new perspective from which to relate to them. It invites us to see them as human beings like ourselves, in need of the same sort of compassion and understanding and care that we desire for ourselves—and then to treat them accordingly. And of course it also turns our attention to life's victims—the wounded, the excluded, the dying—who were always Jesus' particular concern.

The lesson of this parable is no different from the radical teaching of the Sermon on the Mount, in which Jesus calls on us to love our enemies and persecutors and seek their good. Both the parable and Jesus' sermon invite us to see the world through new eyes. To see it as a world transfigured by the utterly inclusive love of God. To see it as Jesus saw it, and to act on that transforming vision as he did.

As we leave behind the bloodiest, most violent and destructive century of all human history, there is no task before us as followers of Jesus Christ, no obligation of faith, no duty to God, more urgent than accepting Jesus' invitation to see—really *see*—our enemies and all whom we are tempted to exclude or despise. To see them as Jesus, our Lord, sees them—as neighbors beloved by God, persons like ourselves. And to treat them accordingly.

9

A Call to Live Jesus' "Impossible Possibility"

Matthew 5:38–45

(PREACHED SEPTEMBER 16, 2001)

You have heard that it was said, "An eye for an eye, and a tooth for a tooth." But now I tell you: do not take revenge on someone who wrongs you. If anyone slaps you on the right cheek, let him slap your left cheek too. And if someone takes you to court to sue you for your shirt, let him have your coat as well. And if one of the occupation troops forces you to carry his pack one mile, carry it two miles. When someone asks you for something, give it . . . when someone wants to borrow something, lend it . . .

You have heard that it was said, "Love your friends, hate your enemies." But now I tell you: love your enemies and pray for those who persecute you, so that you may become the sons [and daughters] of your Father in heaven. For he makes his sun to shine on bad and good people alike, and gives rain to those who do good and to those who do evil. (Matthew 5:38–45, Good News Bible)

THIS PASSAGE FROM THE Sermon on the Mount includes the words of Jesus that were most quoted by Christian writers during the first three hundred years of the church's history. These were the years when Christianity was an illegal religion throughout the Roman Empire and was periodically persecuted, sometimes very savagely. Of all the words of Jesus, these finally impressed themselves on me late last night as the ones we most need to hear and take to heart this first Sunday after the terror of 9/11.

Some years ago, I read them to a group of university students. Afterwards I asked them, "Well, what do you think of that?" My question was greeted with a long, sober silence. One courageous soul finally said,

"It's not possible. It's against human nature." Then more silence, along with a few nods of agreement.

Another student added, "It's a good goal, but nobody does it." Finally a philosophical brother suggested, "It depends on what you mean by love." That gave me a little room to maneuver and get on with the lesson. But the substance of the students' virtually unanimous response was clear: Jesus' teaching about non-retaliation and love of one's enemies is a beautiful ideal; but in the real world, it's impossible.

There has been plenty of evidence during this past week that theirs is still the majority opinion. Retaliation and vengeance are alive and well in our society, in forms as varied as our violent movies, acts of road rage, savage encounters between participants on our TV talk shows, and the speeches of our president and other leaders, religious and political, since last Tuesday's atrocities. There's no lack of public evidence of our society's commitment to retaliation—returning evil for evil—as the necessary, and only honorable, response to those who abuse us.

But Jesus was an honorable man whose teaching on these matters surely deserves a fair hearing in his church. So I want to say a good word for Jesus' "impossible" possibility of non-retaliatory love of one's enemies. For the following interpretations, I am heavily indebted to the inspiring work of theologian Walter Wink.[1]

Our Lord was a marvelously creative teacher who didn't leave his lessons floating around above people's heads in vague abstractions. He gave folks like us word pictures and concrete action stories to help us get his point. In this case, he offers three scenarios to clarify this teaching about non-retaliation and love of one's enemies.

First: *If anyone strikes you on the right cheek, turn the other also.* The picture behind these words is that of a person who holds a superior position in the social order arrogantly humiliating someone whom he considers inferior. This is the kind of backhanded slap by which Jews were put in their place by their Roman overlords in Jesus' day; or by which wives were kept in their place by husbands in that patriarchal society.

Most of Jesus' hearers would probably have loved to slap one of their arrogant Roman rulers just this way. This strike that Jesus pictures is a symbol of domination, an affirmation of who has the upper hand. It's the kind of slap that delivers the message, "I'll teach you who you are: you are a nobody, and don't you forget it!"

So how are followers of Jesus to respond to such bullying? One could accept the humiliating slap as though it were deserved, and then slink—or run—away like a cowed animal. Or one could go after the bully, the way our leaders are promising to go after the terrorists responsible for Tuesday's outrage. Of course, if the social underdog pictured in Jesus' story had taken that course of action and started throwing punches, he would likely have ended up beaten and in jail—or dead. These two possible responses—"flight" and "fight"—are part of our "standard equipment" as human beings. They are our "natural" responses to bullying evil.

But Jesus proposes a "third way" for a victim of the humiliating slap to respond. He advises neither passive acceptance nor aggressive retaliation. Instead, he would have the victim stand there in the oppressor's face, unmoved, and deliberately turn the other cheek. That's a way of saying, "I am *not* your inferior. I do not accept your verdict on my worth. I am a fellow human being, like you, looking you straight in the eye."

Now let's imagine what might happen next. If the bully so chose, he could backhand the victim on that left cheek; but that would require striking with the left hand. The left hand was the hand used in those days of no toilet paper for hygienic purposes. To slap someone with *that* hand would be the sort of unseemly insult that would have been at least as degrading to the slapper as to the one being slapped.

A second alternative for the bully would have been to hit the victim's left cheek with his right hand—administer a right cross, as one would when fighting an equal. But that would be to acknowledge the victim's essential equality, which wouldn't do! Or the bully, in the face of his victim's surprising courage, could back off—or even grudgingly acknowledge her, or his, courage and drop the matter.

So "turning the other cheek" is both self-respecting and respectful of this arrogant "enemy." It is nonviolent, and it creates new possibilities. Read the stories of Jesus' trial and crucifixion in the gospels, if you need help in imagining the power of this kind of response. He faced down all his accusers, did it with dignity and courage to the very end, and then prayed for God to forgive them.

But let's press on now to Jesus' second scenario: *If anyone wants to sue you and take your coat* [your outer garment], *give him your cloak* [your underwear] *as well.* In this case, we are in court. A poor man is being sued by an aggressive creditor who has already taken everything he has except the shirt off his back; and now he demands that. The poor man, like many of the poor in our courts today, is powerless. He has no recourse but to act out: fight—and go to jail—or meekly surrender his robe, which was his principal clothing, as though the creditor's legal claim were just.

But again, Jesus proposes a third, surprising option. Let me paraphrase his words: "So the rascal is taking your outer clothing? Then strip, and give him your underwear, too." Now that's an imaginative response—one that would expose the creditor's heartless greed even more than it exposed the poor man's body. And that's powerful.

But this exposure is nonviolent and—at least as I picture it—a piece of good-natured, almost slapstick, humor. What started as a serious, bullying miscarriage of justice could conceivably end up in a good laugh for all present, except possibly the creditor, if his greed had robbed him of a sense of the ridiculous. Better still, the victim's shocking response could conceivably free this serious banker to enjoy a good laugh, return the man's clothes, and give him time to work out his financial problems. Jesus' proposal, you see, is imaginative and expressive of a completely different spirit than one ordinarily encounters in court.

The third scenario Jesus proposes is based on the Roman law that allowed a Roman soldier to require a Jew, as a colonial subject, to carry his heavy pack a mile. Just one mile—no more. Jesus' answer to this humiliating requirement imposed on his people by their hated oppressors is to astonish the oppressor by offering to carry the pack a second mile at no extra cost! The idea is, treat this enemy like a friend that you've enjoyed helping out, someone you wouldn't mind getting to know better.

Of course Jesus knew that the soldier could be disciplined if he let the man carry his pack more than the legally allowed mile. So this proposed response also takes the initiative and turns the tables on the oppressor. Can't you picture this Roman soldier's embarrassment, and the delight of Jewish bystanders, as he tries to persuade his good-natured victim to give him back his pack before he gets into trouble with his sergeant! So again, Jesus' instruction would turn the tables on an oppressive enemy in a positive, imaginative way that might well give both parties a good laugh.

All three of these scenarios picture nonviolent, creative, disarming resistance to oppressive, bullying behavior. All are calculated to appeal to the oppressor's better side and the better side of Jesus' hearers as well. Jesus is proposing responses to evil that have the potential of uniting victim and victimizer at the level of their common humanity. I'm sure his original hearers found his teaching at least as shocking and "impossible" as we do.

Jesus' examples here remind me of a student anti-war demonstrator's response to an angry, patriotic woman at a Vietnam War protest. She came up to the peaceful demonstrator, got in his face, and loudly called him every bad name in the book. She looked as if she were ready to pounce on him any second and pound him with her pocketbook. When she finally paused to take a breath, he stepped back, looked hurt and shocked, and said, "I heard that." At that, she laughed in spite of herself, and the whole crowd standing around joined her. And that particular little war was over.

That's the spirit—the Holy Spirit—of imaginative good will that Jesus is calling his hearers to embody. I maintain that *it is not impossible* to live his way. It is not only possible, but imperative, that each of us try our best to live Jesus' way in these angry times. His is the reconciling spirit that can free us to identify with our adversaries as human beings, to imagine how it is to sit where they sit and feel what they feel. His Spirit can free us to pray for them and seek their good, to assume the best about them and liberate the best in them, rather than demonizing them as bigots or fools to be ignored or disposed of.

I would go even further than that. I want to propose that this teaching has serious implications far beyond the purely personal level. For example, there was an impassioned public debate a few years ago about whether or not our military should invade Haiti in order to restore order, and encourage some semblance of democracy and peace, there. In a news clip that was broadcast at that time by National Public Radio, peace activist Jim Wallis was being interviewed by a reporter concerning the possibility of such an invasion. They were discussing the complexities of that issue when the reporter impatiently demanded of Wallis, "Well, what should we do—invade or not?"

Wallis replied something like this: "Well, maybe the president should load all the preachers and priests and other religious leaders in the country on Air Force transports filled with money and food and medical supplies for the Haitians, fly the them down there, and let *them* invade Haiti."

Was that a crazy idea? Well, yes. But it was Jesus' peculiar kind of "crazy." And an interesting thing happened: The president did send a former president, Jimmy Carter, accompanied by a senator and an army general, to Haiti in a spirit somewhat like that of Wallis's suggestion, and a bloody invasion was averted.

The point is, Jesus' way of imaginative, nonviolent resistance to evil is the way of hope. It is the only way that can create new possibilities of social and political, as well as personal, healing.

Our addiction to vengeance and war may be satisfied temporarily by violent acts of retaliation. Such acts may even seem to resolve unjust situations for a time. But they will only increase ill will in the long run and set the stage for deepening hatreds and escalating vengeance. We can never establish peace or justice on this tortured earth by means of war. Did we not prove that beyond any reasonable doubt during the twentieth century—the cruelest and bloodiest century of all time?

It is way past time for Christians to get serious about Jesus' way: *no more public or private vengeance; no more violence undertaken to stamp out violence.* This is the moment, for the sake of all future life on earth, to immerse ourselves in the spirit and imagination of Jesus. And to prepare ourselves, as Dr. Martin Luther King and his followers used to do, by prayer and serious training. They did this so that they could stand fearlessly in the face of angry opponents of their civil rights—facing them in a nonviolent spirit of love, seeking always to appeal to the humanity of angry adversaries who were in the grips of hatred and fear.

I am not suggesting—and Jesus never suggested—that his way is guaranteed to make friends of our enemies or to spare us from suffering. Suffering comes with the territory in which broken, sinful humans are to be loved and prayed for, and their healing sought, regardless of their hateful reactions. Human evil is too real and virulent to be confronted in the false hope that by our being kind and imaginative we can always bring a happy ending to situations where there's injustice and oppression and violence. But at the center of our dangerous mission stands Jesus' cross, representing a love that knows no limits, no bounds. And that cross, which stands for the suffering that comes to those who love with the honesty and abandon of Jesus, represents God's promise of victory over all the powers of death and evil in us and around us.

The crucial question before us today is, How might Jesus' way relate to our present situation, as we are under attack from international terrorism? One possibility: Christian peace activists are volunteering to go to Afghanistan and Iraq with medicine, food, and loans to help those wrecked nations and their economies recover from years of terrible war and sanctions. Such a generous offer on the part of large numbers of people of courage and good will would be hard for leaders of those countries to refuse, fearful as their people are of destruction by our powerful military. Their refusal could conceivably cause the leaders to lose face, or even to lose their power. Such a gesture might even show Osama bin Laden and others like him a new face of America—and mitigate their murderous zeal.

A crazy idea? Maybe. But similar efforts by the courageous people of Witness for Peace, who went to Nicaragua in the 1980s during the contra war and stood between the contras and the villagers they were trying to destroy, saved many lives. At the very least, we followers of Jesus can pray for, and think of, the terrorists as our neighbors on this planet earth, whom we are somehow to love as ourselves.

In March of 1989, former President Jimmy Carter essentially did just that when he spoke these words, quoted in the *New York Times*:

> We have only to go to Lebanon, to Syria, to Jordan, to witness first-hand the intense hatred among many people for the United States, because we bombed and shelled and unmercifully killed totally innocent villagers, women and children and farmers and housewives, in those villages around Beirut . . . as a result, we have become a kind of Satan in the minds of those who are deeply resentful. That is what precipitated the taking of hostages and that is what has precipitated some terrorist attacks.

In these words, we see former President Carter trying to put himself in the shoes of the Near Eastern peoples he encountered in his efforts to do humane work in that part of the world. It is significant that he uttered those words before the (first) Gulf War and our terrible bombing of Baghdad, and the awful retribution we have visited on the people of Iraq since that war—blockade and sanctions that have effectively destroyed that society and killed hundreds of thousands of their children. Imagine yourself as an Iraqi mother watching your child waste away and die for lack of medicine that could easily have been available to her—except for the murderous sanctions against her country—sanctions of which the United States has been chief supporter and enforcer.

It is time to take courage, and pray, and use our imaginations, and offer our bodies and resources in taking our Lord's teaching seriously—doing whatever we can to cool the self-righteous war rhetoric around us. We need to understand that behind the inexcusable atrocities of last

Tuesday is a world of genuine hurt and suffering out of which such desperately destructive acts are born. This is not a time to answer hurt and hate and fanatical despair with massive, angry retaliation that can only lead to greater hurt and deeper hate and more entrenched evil.

So let us listen to Jesus' words of hope. Let them sink in and guide our thoughts, our prayers, our imaginations—and all our relationships and communications during this dangerous moment when, for all we know, the future of civilization on this planet as we have known it hangs in the balance. For Christ's sake, let us love our enemies, pray for their good, and in all that we do, act like children of God.

ENDNOTES

1. See Walter Wink's *Engaging the Powers*, 175–89.

A Prince of Peace Who Disturbs Our Peace?

Luke 12:49–56

O NE OF THE FAMILIAR titles of Jesus is the Prince of Peace. He is the one who declared, "Blessed are the peacemakers, for they will be called children of God" (Matthew 5:9). He is the one who assured his followers, "Peace I leave with you; my peace I give to you" (John 14:27). So the words of this gospel reading are troubling, for Jesus says, "Do you think that I have come to bring peace to the earth? No, I tell you, but rather division! . . . [T]hey will be divided: father against son and son against father, mother against daughter and daughter against mother . . ." (Luke 12:51–53).

That just doesn't sound right coming from the Prince of Peace. Some Bible scholars even doubt that these are Jesus' words at all. They think this saying comes from early Christians who were in conflict with unbelievers, and put their feelings into words, and imagined those words to be Jesus' as recorded here by Luke.

Of course that is possible. Anyone who has observed witnesses under pressure, testifying in court, knows that it's not easy to stay clear about exactly who said what, and when. But even if these scholars are right (which I doubt), and even if Jesus never spoke these exact words, they are surely true to his experience. And they are true to the church's experience. For not only in the days of his flesh, but through the centuries, Jesus, the Prince of Peace, has been a cause of division within families, between Christian groups, and among ethnic groups and nations.

Why this strange contradiction: a Prince of Peace who disturbs the peace? Why couldn't Jesus have come and done what one prophet had longed for, "turning the hearts of parents to their children and the hearts of children to their parents" (Malachi 4:6)? Surely *that* is what the world needed then and desperately needs today—not more family conflict, more religious conflict, more division in a tragically divided world.

Why couldn't Jesus have simply loved people, comforted them in their sorrows, healed their diseases, calmed their fears, and brought in the kingdom of peace that the scriptures had promised? Why this contradiction of a Prince of Peace who says, "Do you think I have come to bring peace on earth? No, I tell you, but rather division!" The answer, I believe, lies in another contradiction familiar to us all, illustrated by the following story.

Once there was a youth who greatly desired to be a good and decent man. He married the young woman of his dreams, started a business, and began to raise a fine family. He also began teaching Sunday school at his church and did it with such conviction that he was soon elected an elder. Not long after that, he felt God's call to preach, so he sold his small business, attended seminary, and entered the ministry. And he preached powerfully and passionately.

He preached with special vehemence against lust and fornication and marital infidelity. When his children wanted to learn to dance, he forbade it. When his daughter wanted to become a cheerleader, he refused to allow it. And when her mother sided with her, he was vastly upset and feared for his wife's soul. As the years passed, this man of God became known throughout the community for his determined opposition to the temptations of the flesh.

Then a strange thing happened. It was discovered that he was having an affair with an attractive widow of the congregation. His wife was shattered, his children bitterly hurt, and his friends astonished and disappointed. So his distraught wife confronted him in tears, saying, "How could you *do* such a thing—you, of all people?" At this, he flew into a rage and stormed out of the house. And to this day, he has not forgiven her!

This story has to do with a contradiction we know as well as we know our own hearts. The Apostle Paul spoke of it eloquently: "I do not understand my own actions. For I do not do what I want, but I do the very thing I hate . . . So I find it to be a law that when I want to do what is good, evil lies close at hand. For I delight in the law of God in my inmost self, but I see in my members another law at war with the law of my mind, making me captive to the law of sin which dwells in my members. Wretched man that I am! Who will rescue me from this body of death? Thanks be to God through Jesus Christ our Lord!" (Roman 7:15ff.)

So it is with all of us at one time or another. Like the man in the story, we want to be good and faithful. We struggle to live by what we believe. We hate the weakness in ourselves and the exploitive behavior in others. Yet that hatred is really a reflection of the tragic contradiction in our own souls—a reflection of the infidelity and weakness that we know, hate, and fear in ourselves.

Everyday examples of the contradiction are not hard to find. For example, we parents want our children to know that we love them. We want to be patient and giving with them. Yet in their moments of rebellion and confusion, when they most need our patience and our love, we often find ourselves irritated and frustrated with them, withholding our love and accusing them.

And we children—deep down we want to please our parents. And yet we often find ourselves saying and doing things we know very well will hurt and disappoint them. Or we know we want to make our way in this world honorably, in a manner that will win the respect and love of others. Yet when the hard choices come—between success through cheating or honest failure, between telling the comfortable lie or admitting the embarrassing truth—then too often, I must admit with Paul, "I don't do what I want, but I do the very thing I hate."

God help me. God help us all.

As we know, such contradictions as these are found not only in individual hearts but also at the heart of all of our institutions and communities: the family, the church, the city, the nation, the corporation. Examples abound. A businessman wants his to be a good business that serves the public well, that cares for its own personnel and their families, that contributes to the quality and excellence of the community. But under the pressure of competition, his company can be torn by internal conflict, or shortchange the public, or abuse its personnel and sacrifice its mission and integrity in order to maintain its market share.

Or, we want our church to be faithful to Jesus Christ. We dream of being a source of strength and encouragement to one another and to our neighbors. Yet we become impatient with members who don't exactly share our beliefs and values, we gossip about one another, criticize one another's efforts, and refuse to give the time and energy and money and thought and care required to make the church's dream come true.

There is a contradiction within us, and within all our institutions. We want the good, yet do the very things we hate. God knows it. Jesus knew it. So, yes, Jesus came to bring peace on earth—to deliver us from the contradictions that haunt every one of us and all the enterprises of which we are a part.

But deliverance from a condition so devastating and pervasive can never be easy or cheap. The struggle for liberation from the evil that enslaves us personally and socially inevitably involves heartbreak, suffering, and division. If the Prince of Peace is to bring us real peace, he must expose the contradictions that are robbing us of that peace, and expose himself to the angry denials and hostility of those who are exposed. He must be a disturber of the phony "peace" that is killing us.

This too, we know from our own experience. In the story I told earlier, the man's wife was such a disturber of the peace. She asked an honest, embarrassing question, and he (who surely needed to be forgiven) replied that he would never forgive her for asking!

Haven't we all had to play that kind of painful role on occasion? Have you ever loved someone trapped in self-destructive behavior? A child with a drug problem? A spouse with an alcohol problem? A friend with a personality problem? What happens in those situations when in love you try honestly to help that person confront the contradictory, self-destructive behavior that's wasting her or his life? Answer: the sort of thing that happened in my story when the wife confronted her unfaithful husband.

Vehement denial: "Get off my case! It's my business, I can handle it." Or maybe an angry attempt to blame the questioner: "You're the one with the problem! I'll never forgive you for speaking to me this way! You've ruined our marriage." Sadly, honest words spoken for the sake of peace and healing can become a sword that divides you from the ones you love.

In the face of such responses, those who are trying to help are often tempted to give in to frustration and retaliate, returning anger for anger and blame for blame, and pointing out the stupidity of their loved one's self-defeating behavior. Or if denial and blame continue, would-be helpers are tempted to withdraw and quit trying, saying in effect, "Go ahead, ruin your life. It's your problem. I'm out of here."

But of course neither counterattack nor withdrawal will bring deliverance to your troubled loved one or peace to you. We all know that when we are acting stupidly and hurting ourselves and others, it doesn't seem like "help" when those who love us call on us to face up to the truth of what we are doing. And certainly it doesn't help for them to give up on us and leave us to "stew in our own juices."

When in the name of love and healing, we turn out to be disturbers of the peace of those whom we want to help, and when they deny the truth that's destroying them and turn on us and treat us as enemies, then what? Here is where the Prince of Peace who became a disturber of the peace can show us the way. To begin with, he accepted the inevitability that he would be a disturber of the peace. He knew that his honest disclosure of the contradictions at the heart of people's lives would not be acceptable to them—and in fact, in the end, would offend them all.

In truth, Jesus loved the people of his day far more than they wanted to be loved. He wasn't satisfied to cultivate friendship with the good and respectable folk among them; he befriended the neediest of all: the lost, the sick, the degraded and excluded. When he reached out to these who were so obviously in need of forgiveness and hope, this was especially disturbing to the respectable ones who had settled for a limited notion of God as One who is able to love only "the good and faithful"—i.e., the ones like themselves. So eventually Jesus "disturbed the peace" of all.

In calling all of his people to repentance and faith in God, Jesus was calling them not simply to "save themselves" while the wicked world burned. He was calling them all to their rightful destiny of serving God in the tasks of love by which their wicked, resistant world might be healed. This larger, more gracious calling was what so disturbed the "peace" of Jesus' troubled, fragmented time. It was what so revealed the contradictions in all hearts that, in the end, it brought the people together for a brief moment to rid themselves of this "disturber of their peace."

Jesus knew their hearts, saw how they were responding. And that's why he said, "Do you think that I have come to bring peace to the earth? No, I tell you, but rather division!" His words are the cry of a heart breaking under the recognition that the boundless love he offered, which was their only hope, would create resistance, rejection, and division among those whom he loved so deeply. And so, at the last, when they turned in anger and finally vented their rage against him for loving them and believing in them so much, it was no more than he had expected.

"I have a baptism to be baptized with," he had said in the moment of recognition captured by our text, "and how I am constrained until it is accomplished!" (Luke 12:50)." A baptism to be baptized with"? What is he talking about?

He's talking about the inevitable flood of hatred and hostility that a love as honest and consistent and courageous and broad and deep as his would bring on itself by daring to love *all* the people—including those who were despising one another and hating him. He's talking about baptism in the flood of denial and rejection that troubled people dump on those who love and believe in them, when they no longer believe in themselves. This "baptism" finally engulfed him on the cross because he had dared to love all people with a love big enough and tough enough to embrace their whole contradictory world. A love that absolutely refused to be reduced to a comfortable, inoffensive size.

So who will deliver us from our contradictory selves and our contradictory world? "Thanks be to God, through Jesus Christ our Lord!" exclaimed Paul. He recognized that God alone loves enough—and loves us with a love that is tough enough—to outlast our vehement denials of the truth, our self-doubts, our angry rejections of a Savior's help.

In Jesus, the Prince of Peace, God disturbs our peace only that we may repent and be healed—and find peace. Jesus reveals the divisions among us and the dividedness of our own hearts only in order to bring us a peace that passes understanding. And to transform us after his own likeness into persistent, courageous lovers of our contradictory brothers and sisters and our contradictory human institutions.

He disturbs us for a single purpose: to transform us into prophetic people who care enough to speak honestly to everyone. To speak clearly about the contradictions we see. And about the boundless grace and forgiveness of God, who alone has patience and persistence enough to see us through the failures and pains of our prophetic task, and use us flawed servants in the healing of our tragically confused world.

Thanks be to God for God's tough love revealed so powerfully in Jesus, our Lord!

Tempted to Cop Out? Pray Always!

Luke 18:1–8

*Jesus told them a parable, to the effect that they ought
always to pray and not to lose heart.*

LUKE 18:1

W HY DO YOU SUPPOSE Jesus did that? It seems to me that his followers—people who had seen the blind receiving their sight, the lame
set on their feet, the lepers being healed, and the common people flocking
to him to hear the good news—would hardly have been tempted to lose
heart. Instead, they might have been encouraged as they had never been
encouraged before when they saw God's power at work in this man. So
why would he set about teaching them that they ought always to pray and
not to lose heart?

Surely it was because Jesus realized that tough times were coming—
when the common people would no longer hear him or his followers
gladly, but instead would be crying "Crucify him!" And because the only
thing that kept *him* from losing heart was constant prayer to God, he
believed that was the only thing that could sustain them in the coming days. Certainly their situation was terribly troubled: their nation in
seething resentment against Rome, only forty years before committing
national suicide in a bloody revolt; terrorism raging in the name of the
compassionate God of Israel; family life and morals and the economic
and political situation in terrible shape; and religious fanaticism on the
rise. It was a difficult time, especially for poor and powerless people like
Jesus' followers.

Jesus, better than anyone else, knew that those who take life seriously and who want God's will to be done on this earth are *always* tempted to lose heart. We sinful human beings have a way of undermining our own fondest hopes and dreams of justice and peace. Take the end of the Cold War and the collapse of the Soviet empire, for example—a time so full of hope for a better, more peaceful world in which the resources of the great powers could be devoted to the healing of the nations. It seemed such a promising, fresh beginning, but the world situation is becoming more and more complex and angry and disheartening as the years wear on.

An individual life can be like that, too: full of promise and potential and high hopes at the beginning—only to have those hopes dashed because of a tragic illness or accident, or bad decisions, or lack of educational opportunity. The same with retirement—a time of great hopes and plans in the beginning, but too soon clouded by aches and pains, or serious illness and disability, and the prospect of more to come. Such things can cause us to lose heart. Time and change have a way of wearing down even the most resilient among us. Maybe that's why Jesus told his followers a parable to the effect that they ought always to pray and not to lose heart.

But *always?* Pray *always?* One of the most disheartening features of life today is that the world is so much with us, pressing in from all sides. In this technology- and media-driven age, thoughts of God are so easily crowded out. Everyone is so busy with activities, called on to make so many choices, involved in so much busy work just to keep things going; so busy that there seems to be no time for quiet reflection, for thought, for prayer—much less for praying *always.*

For many people, our situation is too much like that pictured by the philosopher who described us secular-minded moderns as passengers on a runaway train, hurtling through the night while God, the engineer, is dead! The fact is, ours is not a time when many of us find it easy to "pray always"—or to pray very much at all, God help us. Prayer seems so passive, somehow, so devoid of action; and most of us Americans love action.

But the truth is, it wasn't all that easy to pray in Jesus' time either. And that's why he proceeded to tell his followers a little parable about an intrepid widow who pestered a heartless, egotistical judge into giving her justice. What's the point of this parable? Courage and perseverance— against outrageous odds! This woman had no power to influence, nor money with which to bribe this judge, who feared neither God nor humans, and apparently cared little for justice. She, a powerless, victimized woman, had nothing going for her, it seems, except a passionate desire for justice to be done in her case.

Could her name in real life have been Mary of Nazareth, his mother? Jesus' first "prayer mentor"? Who knows? In any case, this courageous woman hounded the judge early and late until he gave up for fear she would finally wear him out. The Greek literally means something like "give him a black eye." Or, as we say nowadays, "scratch his eyes out."

The courageous perseverance of the powerless in the face of callous power—that is the basis of this parable. And it is true to life. This *is* the way that marginal people finally get justice, isn't it? By pestering the powers that be, by wearing them out, by refusing to be denied.

That's the way the Kmart workers finally got a decent contract at their distribution center in Greensboro a few years ago. It was a beautiful thing to see the courage and persistence of those workers; a privilege to be able to stand with them, sing and pray with them outside the Super Kmart store in the cold, until they got their contract. That's the kind of spirit pictured in this parable.

Even so, this woman is a little hard for us to identify with—at least a little hard for me to identify with. I don't like to pester people, and I certainly don't like to beg for anything. It's a weakness, of course. I haven't *had* to pester people to get justice; it came to me easily, because I am a white, educated, privileged male. Sometimes I should have pestered the bullies of this world more on behalf of people like this widow. Sometimes I should have pestered my children more about being the best they could be. Sometimes I should have pestered the saints of the church more about being the church they could have been. Sometimes I should have kicked myself—should kick myself now—for motivation's sake, and for the sake of God's will being done on this earth now.

But then, who wants to be an agitator? Much less a beggar? Not many; not me. Agitators are not all that likable. They are troublesome, irritating. And if they persist, they can get themselves . . . crucified.

No wonder Jesus saw something he liked in this intrepid woman. No wonder he held her up to his disciples, who were inclined to lose their motivation, to lose heart, to quit caring. (No doubt he suffered the same temptation.) Her story is saying that, if this kind of courage and perseverance can cause a complete rascal of a man to do the right thing, how much more will the courageous, passionate, persistent prayers of God's people avail with God, who wants us to have life abundant beyond all we could ask or think? Who wants more than we could ever imagine for the justice and peace of the kingdom of Love to prevail among us? God is at least as open to cries for justice as this sorry judge in the parable was!

So pray, and pray, and pray—courageously, persistently. That's Jesus' point. Don't despair over your life, your marriage, your children, your community, your nation, your world. Don't quit on God. Pray as passionately and persistently as this courageous woman. Claim Jesus' promise that God longs to bless you and your world, longs to respond to your heartfelt prayers.

"Yes," you may object, "but God knows what we need before we ask. Jesus said that too, and warned us against empty, repetitive prayers." And of course it's true: God surely does know our needs before we ask. The real question is, Do *we* know what we need before we ask?

Lots of times I don't know what I think about something important until I get into a passionate discussion of it, and pray and pray over it, and hear myself saying what I think. It is in voicing our desires and hopes that we begin to see them for what they are. Likewise, it is in praying—persisting in prayer for what we believe is right and good and the will of God—that we can come to see the deeper truth of that gracious will and be empowered to go for it.

Like Paul, who three times over was in terrible agonies of prayer, asking God to remove his "thorn in the flesh"—only to find at the last that the thorn was not removed, but rather that God's grace proved sufficient to deal with it. God's grace was greater than he had imagined, and God's answer far greater than his original prayer.

The same was true with our Lord himself, sweating blood in the Garden and crying, "If it be possible . . . take this cup from me . . ."—only to learn that it was *not* possible. And then to be confirmed in his belief that he must die that others might live, and that his dying was the Father's will. So, yes, God knows what we need before we ask, but *we* don't always know. And persistence holds the promise of purifying our prayers of the dross of self-interest and narrow perspectives.

But you may object further, "Yes, I can see that; but isn't it better to work for the kingdom, for justice and peace on earth, than to be praying all the time? Constant prayer seems like a religious cop-out." And so it can be. There is a kind of spiritual otherworldliness that basks in its own spirituality and never quite comes to grips with the struggles and pain of life. But that is not what Jesus has in mind here, surely, and not what he himself showed us.

In fact I would say that often my busyness, my activism, is the real cop-out. To work for peace and justice on earth without persistently, passionately praying "thy will be done" is usually to work for our ideas of God's will, not for that will as it is. It is only through persistent, passionate prayer for God's will—prayer that includes an equally persistent listening for that will, the way Jesus and Paul listened—that we can be delivered from the self-righteousness and cocksure fanaticism that have haunted Christian activism through the ages, and that haunt much of our public life today.

So the point of our Lord's little parable is not that God, like the judge in the story, has to be pestered into submission to *our will*. On the contrary, the only way we know God's will and become fit instruments for God's work on earth is through persistent, continued outpouring of our hearts to the gracious Judge and Savior of us all, whose ways are not our ways, and whose thoughts are not our thoughts. God has ordained prayer as the means whereby our wills and thoughts are purged and brought into harmony with the divine will and are filled with God's power.

Finally, Jesus confronts us in this story with "the indifference of God" to anything less than the best that is in us: our deepest longings, the sincere cries of our heart and soul. These, God honors and uses. But, if I read the parable rightly, God will not be satisfied with our formal and perfunctory praying. A plea for forgiveness that costs us nothing can hardly cleanse our souls. A prayer for one's enemy that is out of touch with the fear and rage that that enemy has stirred up in one's heart is fraudulent.

For God's kingdom to come and God's will to be done on this tortured earth—which is what all honest prayer is about in the end—it is necessary that people like us be grasped by that will and come to want that will more than anything else in all the world. But God will not bludgeon our wills into submission. Instead, God awaits our partnership in the work of salvation—a partnership rooted in and sustained by persistent, empowering prayer.

The problem of our secular age is not that prayer has been tried and found wanting, but that it has too often been found mysterious and demanding and not seriously tried. So Jesus would have us try it, taking a clue from this intrepid woman in his story. He would have us pray, and pray, and pray—with all our heart and soul and mind and strength, with all the persistence and passion of our being—as he did, right down to the bloody sweat in the Garden and the anguished cries from the cross.

The question is not whether God is good or whether prayer makes any difference. The question is whether we will go with Christ into the darkness of our world as he went into the darkness of Gethsemane—and pray, and pray, and pray, and not lose heart. And so his final words in this passage leave each of us with a haunting, deeply personal question: "When the Son of Man comes, will he find faith on earth?" Pray, friends. Pray always, and don't lose heart For God is good, and in God's will is the fulfillment of our lives and hope for this world.

1 2

Jesus' Lonesome Valley—and Ours

Luke 19:28–44, Isaiah 50:4–11: Passion Sunday

THE DEEPER MEANING OF Passion Sunday—or Palm Sunday, as we preferred to call it in my home church—is expressed in the words of this haunting spiritual:

> *Jesus walked this lonesome valley, He had to*
> *walk it by Himself;*
> *O, nobody else could walk it for Him, He had*
> *to walk it by Himself . . .*
> *You must go and stand your trial, You have to*
> *stand it by yourself,*
> *O, nobody else can stand it for you, You have*
> *to stand it by yourself.*

These somber words sound so lonely, so neglectful of the truth of God's presence and the presence of those who love us and help us through life's lonesome valleys. And yet . . . they direct us to the profound challenge of Jesus' Passion for every one of us.

Now you may be thinking, "Why such heavy talk? This is a time to celebrate!" It's true that we love to celebrate on Palm Sunday. It seems so right that Jesus would have been received with shouts of joy and a royal carpet of cloaks and palm branches as he rode into the city on his borrowed donkey. There is something intentionally playful about the whole scene, for this is Jesus' outrageous parody of the triumphal entrances of the "great" leaders of that time, astride their warhorses, followed by their splendid armies and prisoners of war. I'll bet the children in Jesus' unlikely "army" were beside themselves, singing and dancing, all of them enjoying this moment with "King Jesus" on his long-eared charger.

But then . . . the procession crested a hill, and seeing Jerusalem before him, Jesus was suddenly reminded of what inevitably lay in store for the city. And he wept, crying out to Jerusalem, "Would that even today you knew the things that make for peace! But now they are hidden from your eyes. For the days shall come upon you, when your enemies will . . . surround you, and hem you in on every side, and dash you to the ground, you and your children within you, and they will not leave one stone upon another in you; because you did not know the time of your visitation from God" (Luke 19:41–44).

Can you imagine it? Jesus amidst that excited crowd that can hardly wait for him to get on with the business of delivering them from all their enemies—suddenly bursts into tears! Why? Because he well knew the terrible price his people must one day pay for their misguided patriotism, their seething hatred of their enemies, and their fanatic faith—all of which were driving them to a suicidal revolt against Rome that could only bring utter destruction to their city, and their temple, and their life as a nation. He realized that they didn't know, and wouldn't listen to, the things that make for peace—and that would be their undoing. But they couldn't see it, and he knew they would turn on him for saying it. So he wept—even as the hosannas were ringing in his ears.

In all this, Jesus' experience was remarkably like that of the prophet whose words are recorded in the fiftieth chapter of Isaiah. Let's remind ourselves of the historical situation to which these words were originally directed. The troublesome little kingdom of Judah had been utterly defeated by the Babylonians, and its ablest citizens carried away to exile in Babylon, where their conquerors hoped they would forget about their God and the notions of freedom and justice and trust in God that had made them such a thorn in the flesh of the powerful empires that had tried to control them over the years.

This anonymous prophet tells us how God had given him "the tongue of those who are taught"—that is, the message of one attuned not to the clamorous voices that keep society in an uproar, but to the quiet, mysterious voice of the Spirit who teaches God's messengers how to sustain people wearied and burdened by the incessant conflicts and enticements of the world around them. Morning by morning God opened this man's ear, he tells us—wakened him to hear messages of hope—real hope—for the weary Judean exiles. But it turned out that his people didn't want to listen to such messages.

And why didn't they? Because the Babylonians' imperial strategy for subduing these captives was apparently working. God's prophet was calling them to wake up from the world of their captivity and leave Babylon, and go back home to Jerusalem to claim their promised destiny under God. He was calling them to accept God's forgiveness for the senseless sins that had led to their downfall, and to accept God's gift of a glorious new future of faithfulness and service as a "light to the nations."

But . . . many of them had learned to feel at home in Babylon. Not a few had good jobs there; they had adjusted and were doing quite well, thank you. They "had become acculturated," as we say these days. Besides, the gods of Babylon—gods that certainly seemed to be bringing their worshipers power and success—were not demanding and meddlesome like the God of Israel. The Babylonians would polish up their giant idols, load them on floats and parade them through the streets whenever they needed to whip up religious enthusiasm for this or that imperial adventure. And these handsome gods never said a mumblin' word of protest; and never passed judgment on their owners or stirred up prophets to deliver disturbing messages about justice and the plight of the poor and oppressed, the way Israel's invisible God did.

In short, the exiles had become comfortable with their new situation and its benefits, including the gods that it provided to bless their successes and meet their religious needs. So the acculturated exiles who were living the "good life" in Babylon predictably rejected the prophet's message. Some even went so far as to ridicule and humiliate and spit on him for delivering it.

But now comes the surprising part. He accepted their abuse; he even took their rejection to be an inevitable part of his mission. Through it all he continued to listen for God's word and to speak what he heard to a people so dead to the true calling and promise of their lives that they not only shut their ears to the message, they attacked the messenger. In the face of this lonely trial, the prophet says,

> *The Lord God has opened my ear,*
> *and I was not rebellious,*
> *I didn't turn back.*
> *I gave my back to those who struck me,*
> *and my cheeks to those who pulled out my beard;*

I did not hide my face
from insult and spitting.
The Lord God helps me;
therefore I have not been disgraced;
therefore I have set my face like flint,
and I know that I shall not be put to shame;
[God] *who vindicates me is near.* (Isaiah 50:5–8a)

Is it any wonder that we read this passage on Passion Sunday? It is astonishingly like Jesus' story, isn't it? Jesus must surely have taken courage from the experience of this servant of God of a former generation who, like himself, had been given a message of comfort and hope for the weary and heavy laden, and had been rejected by the very ones he sought to help.

And notice: this passionate prophet (again, like Jesus) didn't hesitate to invite others to follow in his lonely way. Listen to him:

Who among you fears the Lord
and obeys the voice of his servant
who walks in darkness
and has no light,
yet trusts in the name of the Lord
and relies upon his God?

Jesus clearly accepted that challenge, still trusting and crying out to God to the very end, when it seemed that even God had abandoned him. It was then that he shouted, "My God, my God, why have you forsaken me?" (Mark 15:34) Not only so, but like the prophet, Jesus had offered the challenge of his own painful experience to his followers: "If any want to become my followers, let them deny themselves and take up their cross and follow me. For those who want to save their life [that is, who cling to the status or comfort or privileges of their present life situation] will lose it, and those who lose their life for my sake, and for the sake of the gospel [that is, those who renounce their addiction to their personal status quo for the sake of delivering the message of hope and healing that they have heard from Jesus] will save it" (Mark 8:34–35).

To be specific—if we, like Jesus, are faithful as bearers of God's healing truth to people rendered blind and deaf by the attractions of "the good life," then, like him, we must bear our cross and walk our lonesome valley. Others can't walk it for us.

Let me be even more specific. When God opens your ears to the Good News of comfort and hope and deliverance for the victims of this world—both the down and out and the comfortably acculturated—and when you and I begin to speak and act out Jesus' passionate love for the poor, and the oppressed, and the prisoners, and the excluded, including our enemies, saying and doing things that cause our comfortable and prosperous friends to get uneasy or angry at us, or even to accuse us of being do-gooders, or radicals, or terrorists, or religious fanatics, or dangerous fools—then we will be in a position to understand and embrace this ancient prophet's message of encouragement for those who walk the lonesome valley of rejection. This is the path that Jesus walked, and the one that he invites us to follow.

Like Jesus, we don't have to turn back or get bitter and defensive when folks we love and try to help don't accept the message we bring. We just need to keep listening for God's message ourselves; listening and growing in our understanding of it, and in our obedience to it, and in patiently sharing it with the weary, hungry folk to whom God sends us. God will help us, and will not abandon us.

So the ancient challenge stands: Who among you fears the Lord and obeys the voice of his servant, who walks in lonely darkness for the sake of God's life-giving message, yet trusts in God? God knows, such courageous servants are needed now as never before.

I'm thinking of compassionate servants like those who keep reminding us that half of humankind is undernourished or starving, while we waste food and fight our battles against obesity. I'm thinking of the troublesome environmentalists who keep on reminding us that our frantic pursuit of wealth is poisoning the air and waters and lands of our burdened planet and destroying its other species at a terrible rate. And oh, how we need the blessed peacemakers who never tire of reminding us that the weapons we keep making and selling and stockpiling and using on others will one day be used on us as surely as we continue such madness.

We desperately need passionate souls who will risk their neighbors' wrath by relentlessly reminding us and our leaders that we and our nation will be destroyed as surely as Jerusalem and her children were destroyed, if we fail to recognize the opportunity God is giving us *now* to forsake our trust in violence and war and wealth and domination. Souls who invite us to embrace Jesus' call to pursue the things that make for peace, whether here or in Iraq and Afghanistan or the other places where we are throwing our imperial weight around.

But of course everyone's ears aren't attuned to national and global issues.

So God also awakens the ears of other servants to the more personal messages of comfort and healing truth that must be heard and spoken. Messages delivered for the sake of peace in our marriages and family relationships, where denial of the painful truth of past abuse and neglect destroys hopes for love and reconciliation in the future. Messages delivered for the sake of peace in our work relationships, where the denial of a living wage and decent health care to indispensable workers and their families creates conditions of deprivation and resentment and crime that threaten us all. Messages delivered for the sake of peace in our congregations and communities where truth denied and distorted in the past poisons our future together.

These are the ordinary, everyday settings where weary captives of evils denied and unforgiven must be liberated—"born again" and united in Jesus' Spirit of honest speaking and mutual respect, of simple justice and forgiveness, of peace with God and with one another. Of course, the passionate souls who urge people to this kind of radical personal and relational transformation will inevitably encounter the same kind of blindness and deafness and hostility that Jesus and the prophets had to endure. But that's okay; it goes with the territory—a territory where there are not only resisters to the messages we are to deliver, but sisters and brothers who are drawn by the Spirit to walk with us and encourage us.

So here's the challenge of Jesus' passion to each of us: Let God open your ears morning by morning to the Good News of Jesus' unrelenting, transforming love, which holds the promise of life's highest joy for us all. And then speak and do what God gives you to say and do. Some will reject your efforts and turn on you in anger, and reduce you to tears again and again. But don't turn back. For no one else can speak and act for you; you must do it yourself—for the sake of those weary, resistant ones for whom it can yet become the very bread of life. But also for the sake of fellow servants who need the encouragement of your love and fidelity to Jesus' way as they struggle with rejection and discouragement in pursuit of the calling which all of us share.

And always be assured, fellow servants: Jesus, who walked this lonesome valley, has promised to walk it with us all our days—until our word is spoken and our work is done. We can depend on that.

13

A Vulnerable, Suffering God

Mark 15:34

PICTURE IT THE WAY Mark tells it. Darkness at noon for three terrible hours—a sign of the end of the world. Then Jesus' shouted prayer, "My God, my God, why have you forsaken me?"

The bystanders misunderstood, as they had misunderstood so much about this man. Misconstruing his words as a plea to the ancient prophet, one ran and filled a sponge with sour wine, put it on a stick and gave it to him to assuage his pain, saying, "Wait, let's see if Elijah will come and take him down." Then came another agonizing shout as Jesus breathed his last.

That's Mark's chilling picture of the final minutes. But the most chilling moment of all is that heart-freezing cry, "My God, my God, why have you forsaken me?" What are we to make of it? How can one even presume to speak of it?

Commentary on such a scene verges on sacrilege, because here we enter into Jesus' Holy of Holies—far beyond our depths, far beyond our capacity to comprehend. And yet we must try; because these words bring us face to face with a stark alternative: either Jesus' Good News of God was a cruel delusion, or here, in the depths, we encounter the very heart of the gospel, the very heart of God.

Think for a moment about that first alternative: the tragic possibility that Jesus' splendid vision of the kingdom of God was a delusion. It certainly looked that way when he uttered his terrible cry. The crowds of poor people—the sick, crippled, demon-possessed folk who had heard him so gladly, sought his help so urgently—were now gone; or if present, they were silent. The righteous accusers who had dogged his steps, challenging, criticizing, looking for any opportunity to bring him down, had finally succeeded and were there to mock him in his final agony.

Pilate, though hardly convinced that Jesus was a real threat to Roman power, had been more than willing to execute him on the chance that he might be more dangerous than he seemed. The powerful prefer to be safe rather than sorry. Meanwhile, of his chosen disciples to whom Jesus had entrusted his mission and opened his heart, one had betrayed him, another denied him, and the rest deserted him—except for a few faithful women, who watched on helplessly.

Here he was, enduring the most painful death imaginable, surrounded by mocking, uncomprehending enemies, knowing that his bewildered, defeated followers were out there somewhere, with nowhere to go and no one to lead them. All of his hopes and dreams for them and for God's kingdom on earth were seemingly at an end. He had given all he had to give, and now he was dying. And from the One whom he called "Father"? No word, no sign; only darkness and silence.

Sailors in the submarine service have an expression "crush depth." That's the depth at which the underwater pressure is too great for a submarine's hull to withstand, and it is crushed. Here we encounter Jesus at "crush depth." We can only imagine what he experienced, what he wondered. Had his demonstration of the kingdom of God been based on a delusion? A delusion born of the desperate predicament of his people? A delusion born of his own passionate longing for God to heal the people's suffering and sin?

Could it be that there was, after all, no "good news for the poor" and the sick and the excluded? No release for the prisoners of evil? No recovery of sight for those blinded by their own hardness of heart? No chance of God's will being done "on earth as it is in heaven"? Had his own excessive hopes and dreams, rather than God, led Jesus into confrontation with the authorities, into the hell of these last few hours?

Or worse, had God in fact led him into this hell of pain and rejection, only in the end to abandon him? Where now was the One he called Father—the one completely faithful Companion of all his days? Surely he must have wondered, must have longed for some sign of divine approval or vindication; else why this anguished scream of a prayer?

But it was not to be. And with another wordless shout, he died— crushed. How are we to escape the terrible conclusion that his dream of

God's kingdom—of beloved community on earth as it is in heaven—was in fact a delusion?

Mark would have us consult the scriptural source of Jesus' words here. His anguished cry comes not only from the heart, but from the twenty-second Psalm. It begins with this cry of abandonment but ends with an affirmation of confidence in the fulfillment of God's purpose of deliverance, not only for forsaken sufferers like the psalmist—and Jesus—but for all who are in need of God's deliverance: "all the families of the nations" (Psalm 22:27). This scriptural connection implies that Jesus' abandonment is (as Mark sees it) actually the prelude to God's victorious liberation of all!

Further, in order to help us grasp the significance of Jesus' dying, Mark offers us two cryptic bits of commentary that point to its deepest meaning. First, he notes that far from Calvary, the curtain of the Temple, which blocked the way to the Holy of Holies and supposedly hid the face of God, is ripped in two from top to bottom at the instant of Jesus' death (Mark 15:38). Second, Mark reports that at that same moment, Jesus' Roman executioner, who stands facing the cross, is so moved by the manner of his victim's dying that he exclaims, "Truly this man was God's Son!" (Mark 15:39).

So when Jesus breathes his last, the temple veil, which had, in effect, hidden the mystery of God from the people for ages, is torn away from the top down, as though by the very hand of God. And simultaneously a Roman soldier, of all people, sees something powerfully godlike in this dying man. And these things are somehow related to Jesus' terrible cry, "My God, my God, why have you forsaken me?"

What can they mean? I take them to be Mark's way of declaring that this God who was invisible *to* Jesus in the depths was nevertheless visible *in* Jesus—visible in some measure even to his pagan executioner. The invisible God of Israel had escaped the holy place behind the temple veil (God's "proper" place) and moved into the streets, to this public place of state-sanctioned murder, and had at last become visible in this dying man—visible for all the world to see. Even his bloody-handed Roman executioner could see God in this "godforsaken" man! Such is Mark's testimony.

So what kind of God did the soldier see? A vulnerable, forsaken, suffering, dying God; for that's all there was to see. The God revealed in the face of Jesus on the cross is not like the invulnerable, dominating God who dwells in the minds and imaginations of the comfortably "saved"—a

God whose role is to punish the disobedient and bless believers from on high. In fact, it was in defense of their belief in a righteous, exclusive, omnipotent, judgmental God that Jesus' pious adversaries had him crucified. I think they probably did it with a good conscience, the way righteous people today condemn those whom they judge to be unrighteous and unbelieving and hell-bent for destruction.

The righteous, exclusive "God" of people's religious imaginations would long since have forsaken Jesus. After all, Jesus broke Sabbath rules for the sake of sick and hungry and demon-possessed people; he forgave offenders without the benefit of priest or sacrifice; he defiled himself by keeping company with sinners and outcasts and "improper" women—even with violent revolutionaries, like the ones crucified with him on his left and his right. No, the God visible in the crucified Jesus was not the righteous judge who rescues the "righteous" and condemns the rest.

The God revealed in the face of Jesus on the cross is not a god of "might makes right." On the contrary. It was in the name of such a god, the god of the Roman legions, that the executioners did what they did to Jesus. I'm quite sure they did it believing it was their duty to the "divine" emperor of their mighty empire. The gods of power and domination had obviously forsaken Jesus. They were on the other side; or else, like Rambo, they would most surely have zapped Jesus' tormentors and delivered him from the cross.

The false gods of righteous religious exclusivism and dominating power have nothing to offer people whom life has brought to crush depth, because that's not where they hang out. Those gods can be found in comfortable sanctuaries and proper prayers and uplifting music and inspirational spiritual experiences and hard-hitting sermons against the sins of the unrighteous (i.e., those "other people" who don't think, look, act, or believe like us saved folk here in the sanctuary). When these judgmental gods of the righteous are found around people who are operating at crush depth, they are more likely to support the crushers than the crushed—just the way they did at Calvary.

Likewise, the false gods of power, wealth, and success hang out in the hearts and haunts and portfolios of the mighty, in the military forces and the weapons and torturers and executioners who do their dirty work. And they unfailingly side with the winners and crushers—not the crushed.

But these gods of religious rectitude and dominating power are not the God on whom Jesus called in his death agony, for they had long since forsaken him, and he them (See the Temptation story: Matthew 4:1–11; Luke 4:1–13). No, the One on whom Jesus called in the terrifying forsakenness of his dying was somehow accessible even at crush depth—was there *for* him, and *in* him, even though hidden from him at that moment by his mortal anguish. Else why would Jesus have prayed at all?

This is what the soldier dimly saw—and what Mark surely wants us to see—in Jesus' dying. It is what Mark's powerful story is inviting all the world to see. In Christ Jesus, and him crucified, God is so completely identified with all who are being crushed by the powers of evil that it can truly be said that in him this tortured world's vulnerable Creator suffers our forsakenness, our anguish, our dying.

On the cross God, the One whom Jesus called Abba, Father, was crushed for us; revealed as a God who suffers the full weight and tragedy of the human situation. He died *with* us and *for* us. As Jesus had embodied the limitless compassion and healing power of God in his life, so in his death he embodied the depth of God's vulnerable, suffering, love that is deeper than all our pain and failure.

Jesus dying in agony on the cross is the heart of his revelation of God. We are told that Martin Luther, as he contemplated Jesus on the cross, cried, "This man is *God*! This *God* is man!" Walter Wink writes:

> As the Crucified, Jesus . . . *identifies with every victim of torture, incest, [racism], or rape; with every peasant caught in the cross fire of enemy patrols; with every single one of the forty thousand children who die each day of starvation. In his cry from the cross, "My God, my God, why have you forsaken me?" he is one with all doubters whose sense of justice overwhelms their capacity to believe in God; with every mother or father who cradles the lifeless body of a courageous son or daughter; with every Alzheimer's patient slowly losing the capacity of recognition. In Jesus we see the suffering of God with and in suffering people.*[1]

What we see in Jesus means we can push out into the deep with him, trusting in the care of our vulnerable Creator, and give ourselves for the sake of the healing and liberation of all the broken, suffering victims of the false gods that terrorize our world. We need not fear to give ourselves to Jesus' continuing, dangerous work of compassion and justice and peace on earth, for the living and true God will *not* abandon us, even in our moments of utter despair and forsakenness—even at crush depth. Though we die, yet shall we live, as God lives, as Jesus lives. The living and true

God's strength is made perfect in the seeming weakness of nonviolent self-giving and sacrifice, not in violence and domination.

And so, with the Apostle Paul, "I am convinced that neither death, nor life, nor angels, nor rulers, nor things present, nor things to come, nor powers, nor height, nor depth, nor anything else in all creation, will be able to separate us from the love of God in Christ Jesus our Lord" (Romans 8:38–39). Jesus sets us free—free to live; free to die; free to speak and to stand for the truth of God's boundless love, whatever the cost.

Thanks be to God!

ENDNOTES

1. Wink, *Engaging the Powers*, 142.

14

Jesus' Resurrection Makes All the Difference

Luke 24:1–12; Acts 10:34–43

CHRISTIANS ARE ALWAYS IN the season of Easter, which is not about new clothes and bunnies and eggs, or even about the miraculous awakening of the natural world. Christianity, and Easter, are about Jesus of Nazareth, who was crucified and was raised from the dead! Without the resurrection of Jesus after his death on the cross, there would be no Christian faith. The resurrection made all the difference. That's what we celebrate.

There never has been, and probably never will be, a broad agreement among Christians as to what, exactly, happened on that third day after Jesus died. Or on those other occasions the New Testament tells about, when the risen Lord made himself known to his disciples. That's because what happened was beyond the power of the human senses fully to grasp and of human words fully to describe. But this much is clear: without those mysterious happenings to which the gospel witnesses bear their often confusing testimony, there would have been no New Testament, no Christian faith, and no Christian church.

Without his resurrection, the movement Jesus started was thoroughly discredited, its leader disgraced, dead and buried. With the resurrection, the transforming significance of Jesus' shameful death was revealed, and his life and ministry vindicated and continued by an astonishing act of God—no less. The resurrection made all the difference!

Now let's admit right here that for many honest souls, maybe for all of us at one time or another, the resurrection of Jesus presents real problems. It is strange to our world and difficult to reconcile with most of our society's ideas of reality. How much easier it is to get hold of Jesus' parables and his call to love God and our neighbors, and his marvelous example of courage and fidelity to his calling, even to death.

That such a good and courageous man would be executed in this angry world is not at all surprising to those of us who survived the twentieth century, the bloodiest of human history. But that one such victim of injustice was raised from the dead by our Creator, made himself known to his followers, rallied them and sent them forth as witnesses to his story in all the world? That just doesn't fit into the experience and the picture of reality that most people in our society share. It is a strange doctrine to modern ears and a stumbling block to many—even to many who love Jesus.

But this is just the point. What we modern folk fail to remember is that Jesus' resurrection was no less a problem for his original disciples than it is for us. In fact it was probably more of a problem for them than for us. The gospels describe them as being "perplexed," "alarmed," even "terrified" by their experience of it.

Luke says that when the women came from the tomb and told the other disciples their story, it seemed to them "an idle tale, and they did not believe them." And when Peter went and checked it out, he was "amazed." But why wouldn't they be amazed and alarmed? Especially Peter. Put yourself in their place, and remember what they had just been through.

In the garden when Jesus was arrested, some of his followers had been willing to defend him, but he would have none of it—leaving them either to join him or to save themselves, which they did by running for their lives. He had continued in his refusal to defend himself during his phony trial before the Jewish leaders. After that, even Peter finally panicked and denied even knowing him. That left Jesus absolutely alone during his trial before Pilate, and afterwards when the soldiers stripped and whipped and humiliated him with their cruel crown and mock homage. With his few remaining friends standing at a safe distance, he had been executed in the cruelest, most shameful manner available—the method reserved by the Romans for rebels and slaves.

Now if you had been one of the disciples who had boasted with Peter that they would die with him before they would deny him, would you have wanted to look Jesus in the eye again? Jesus, risen from the dead? In their place I think I might have been relieved never to see him again, God help me. So it's no wonder they were amazed and terrified at the news that he had been raised up by God and was alive.

We in this modern age tend to have trouble with the idea of the resurrection and its strangeness to our way of thinking. But what bothered them was the frightening experience of it. This friend whom they had forsaken to a horrible death was alive in a strange new way. For them that was not a doctrine but a shocking happening that changed everything for them forever.

It was the unbelievably gracious experience of his returning to them, not in condemnation but in forgiveness and peace, that shattered the darkness of his death and their own terrible failure, and finally brought into focus what had been happening when Jesus walked among them. In the hearts of those discredited disciples, startled and terrified; in the heart of Peter, brokenhearted over his unforgivable cowardice; in the hearts of the amazed women at the empty tomb; in the hearts of all the astonished witnesses—to all these, the risen Lord's appearance to them overcame mountains of guilt and shame and fear, and kindled fires of faith and courage and compassion that all the power and cruelty of the ancient world were helpless to extinguish.

It was the encounter with the risen Lord that made the difference. Before the resurrection, we have Jesus of Nazareth, a charismatic Jewish prophet, teacher, healer, and exorcist who created enormous excitement among the common people, but whose life and movement were seemingly snuffed out and discredited by his humiliating and shameful death. After the resurrection, we have the movement reborn, with Peter—pitiful, discredited Peter—now boldly announcing to the people that Jesus is "Lord of all . . . the one ordained by God as judge of the living and the dead"(Acts 10:42).

Before the resurrection, we see forlorn, brokenhearted, fearful disciples, hiding behind closed doors, guilty, silent, disorganized. Afterwards we see Peter standing before the very same authorities that had engineered Jesus' death and saying to their faces, "Jesus Christ of Nazareth, whom you crucified . . . God raised from the dead" (Acts 4:10). And we find people who were supposed to be seen, not heard—women like Mary Magdalene and Joanna and Mary the mother of James—testifying to the resurrection with startling courage. The resurrection made all the difference.

Jesus lives—that's the point. He is more alive, more powerful in my life than any other person I have ever known. And he is present here, now, not because we invited him; not because we are worthy of his presence; not because we have "believed" as sincerely as we should, much less honored and served him as he deserves.

In fact, if we take Jesus seriously, we must conclude that the God and Father of our Lord Jesus Christ is not primarily concerned about being served by us; God wants to serve us and to empower us to serve one another. If God is as Jesus showed God to be, then God is not interested in being exalted but is willing to take the lowest place—the place of a servant without any rank or status—for the sake of those without rank or status in this world's pecking order.

God, as Jesus revealed God, is far less concerned about being properly feared and celebrated than about being recognized and known in the "least" among us—known as their inseparable companion in their sufferings. This God wants us to know that as we serve them, we serve God. This God embodied in Jesus is not relaxing in some heavenly suburb, divinely indifferent and detached. This God is to be found in the midst of the "war zones" of our cities, working to realize beloved community where it is most desperately needed. This compassionate God is irrevocably committed to human liberation—to the struggle against every social and political and spiritual evil that holds humankind captive and robs people of courage and hope, and love and joy in life.

The message of the resurrection is that God, the Creator and Sustainer of all that is, is like Jesus. The judge of the living and the dead is on our side (not on the side of our kind of people *only*: believers like us, our family, race, class, party, religion, nation). The judge is on the side of suffering humanity, all of us prisoners—on our side when we are most lost and least lovable, at our side in the form of the least and lost sisters and brothers whom we befriend in his spirit.

This judge of the living and the dead is none other than the eternal "attorney for the defense"—Jesus, who gave his life for the release of all the prisoners of sin and evil. This judge is not interested in deciding between the worthy and the unworthy, between those who are more guilty and those who are less guilty. All are guilty, God knows, and all are infinitely loved; and all are in need of a new start, and a transformed life.

This judge of the living and the dead offers mercy, forgiveness, and reconciliation to all. Why? Because God wants to give us back our future—wants to free us from our crippling past.

Think about it. Do we find Peter and the others after that first Easter eaten up by guilt and remorse, ceaselessly dwelling on their earlier blindness and cowardice? No, we see them freely acknowledging their past failures but never dwelling on them. They are moving on, boldly living in the forgiveness of their living Lord, whose continuing work—in spite of their failures—he had commissioned them to do. They had learned, as we must all learn, that there is more mercy in Jesus Christ than there is sin in us, or in the whole world. Like them, we are to live courageously in that mercy.

The deepest truth of our lives is that we have been raised from death and captivity to evil—raised to a bold and gracious new life with Jesus Christ. Like Paul, we have been crucified with Christ and live now a new life of trust in Jesus, a life empowered by his risen presence within and among us. Under the powerful influence of his Spirit in us, the lingering power of our prejudices and fears is being broken.

Granted, we live in a world in which different spirits are still powerfully at work and seem to be in charge; and from time to time we surrender to those oppressive spirits, God forgive us. But at heart we are a new people through the risen presence of Jesus, a presence deeper and broader and more powerful than all the powers of death within and around us. We are a new community called to trust God and to care in a world where caring is penalized; called to be open and compassionate to all sorts and conditions of people in a world where that makes the authorities anxious at best, and at worst, furious and murderous toward us.

In such a world, we are Jesus Christ's courageous people, being freed to become more and more like Jesus, our Lord, every day. So when it seems that we are hemmed in by sick customs and bad habits, by traditions and prejudices, and by our own fears and memories of how weak and vulnerable we are; when it seems that we are powerless victims of the callous institutions and impersonal powers of our society—we are to remember Jesus, risen from the dead, the firstborn of a new creation—and press on to the tasks in which he leads us.

Our religion is a religion of miracle. We are not shut in to expecting and reenacting the same old destructive soap opera. We are children of the resurrection, living in a world open to the life-giving, transforming power of God.

All the forces of evil—all the forces of death—have met their match in Jesus of Nazareth. In that broken, beaten, forsaken brother and lover of us all, every bit of the love of God that could be poured into a mortal human life engaged the powers of death without resorting to their tactics. And the powers did their worst.

Working in people like us, the powers of death killed him, said *No!* to God's forgiving love. "Were you there when they crucified my Lord?" asks the old spiritual. And my answer is, "Yes, I was there in those who did that deed. I'm a child of this world who resists the love of God. Yes, I was there in them. But I was also there in Jesus, who embraced in his everlasting love the world that put him there; who loved us all to the very end and gave himself for us all."

And that unconquerable love prevailed. God said *Yes!*—raised Jesus from the grave and turned his fearless, compassionate Spirit loose in the world to recreate it as the beautiful beloved community it was intended to be.

I do believe he is performing his miracle of new creation even now, even in me, and in you, and in every faithful effort to encourage trust in God and establish God's justice and peace in this torn world—thanks be to God! In such deeds of faith and hope and love, Jesus lives. And because he lives, we also shall live.

15

Jesus' Way with the Alienated

John 21:15–19

W HAT IS A SOCIETY to do with those who are a part of it but deeply
alienated from it? What about our neighbors who lack the opportunities and skills to participate and succeed in it? Neighbors who have
been shut out of its benefits and privileges so long that they have lost
hope? Neighbors for whom the police and the courts are more of a threat
to their safety and peace than a defense against crime and injustice?

I'm talking about those trapped in poverty, about minority groups
victimized by the racism and classism and economic injustice that afflict
those who struggle at the socioeconomic bottom of American society.
Their plight was graphically symbolized and widely publicized by vivid
pictures of the savage beating of Rodney King at the hands of Los Angeles
police officers.

Among the poor and excluded there are, by the grace of God, many
who trust God and keep faith with one another and, as they are able, keep
faith with the larger community that rejects and exploits them. They care
for their own with the extraordinary heroism of the faithful poor, and
they are remarkably free of bitterness toward the rest of us. They know
and feel the injustice of their situation and hate it, but miraculously it
doesn't destroy their souls.

Among them are not a few saints and many courageous souls struggling for justice and peace. Some of these may have worked for you in your
business, cared for your children, cleaned your homes or your church, or

loved and cared for your ill elderly. If you were of a mind to listen and care, you may have heard and felt their pain and seen their tears over children and other loved ones lost to drugs or prison or violence. I thank God for the many courageous saints among the alienated. They hurt terribly, but incredibly they don't take it out on others; so the rest of us are inclined to ignore the depth of the injustice of their suffering, even as we trust them—and use them.

There are also many exceptionally capable and energetic individuals who are highly successful in society in spite of the discrimination they regularly experience. Many of them overcome the circumstances that defeat others, and many of these never look back. But others, like Martin Luther King and my friends, Nelson and Joyce Johnson, devote their lives to helping others to break free, thanks be to God.

Even so, the poorest of the poor and the angriest of the alienated are trapped, usually in our inner cities, ready to explode in fury when provoked. Many such neighbors have come to believe that they can never have a decent life on our society's terms, so they reject its terms. So how is a society to deal with those who are most alienated from it? And how are the followers of Jesus to respond to this urgently important part of God's call to beloved community?

Society's age-old way of dealing with its victims is the way of suppression: resort to the use of force and punishment to control or eliminate those among the alienated who, in the opinion of the ruling powers, pose a threat to the rest of society. Pharaoh is the prime example of this method in the Bible. The Israelite slaves in Egypt were a growing, alienated underclass. They made Pharaoh nervous. What, he fretted, if their hardy population kept growing at a rate far exceeding that of the Egyptians? And what if enemies appeared on Egypt's borders, and the Israelites sided with those enemies against the Egyptians?

For the peace and welfare of Egypt, Pharaoh concluded that this growing menace had to be controlled. He committed himself, his authority, and all necessary force to subdue the Israelite slaves. Oppressive enforced labor, covert and overt genocide, and military action—Pharaoh was willing to use them all. Whatever it took. His approach was classic.

Similar tactics were used by our ancestors against Native Americans. And virtually all of Pharaoh's methods, and a number of others, have been used in the South against African Americans. Even more murderous, refined techniques were used by Nazi Germany against the Jews of Europe.

Ruling elites have used them for years (with American support) in Central and South America to control the masses of that region. Whatever it takes to control the alienated and recalcitrant—that's the rule, in the name of order and stability

In recent years, "preemptive" suppression has been the plan at home and abroad: stricter laws, zero tolerance, more arrests, speedier trials, stiffer sentences, fewer paroles, more and bigger prisons, and more executions to control the situation at home, along with "police actions" and wars on foreign soil. So when Rodney King appeared threatening and recalcitrant, the police were prepared—seemingly eager—to do whatever it took to subdue him. It was ugly on video, and it made the alienated furious. The rest of us were mostly ashamed or afraid. The police action that day was clearly excessive, but it was true to the classic approach.

We shouldn't have been shocked when middle-class jurors empathized with the frightened police officers and acquitted them of any wrongdoing. And certainly we shouldn't have been shocked when the alienated of Los Angeles and other urban centers responded with self-destructive looting and violence. Neither should any have been shocked when President George H.W. Bush ordered 4,500 armed troops into L.A. the Friday night after the verdicts and vowed "to use whatever force is necessary to restore order." Once again, the classic formula!

"Viewed from outside the trial, it was hard to see how the verdict could possibly square with the video," admitted the president. Yet he continued, "We must respect the process of law whether or not we agreed with the outcome. In a civilized society there can be no excuse—no excuse—for the murder, arson, theft, and vandalism that have terrorized the law-abiding citizens of L.A."

With this, then Governor Bill Clinton of Arkansas heartily agreed. "I think the president did a good job tonight, taking the steps he should have," said Clinton. Then he added (perhaps for voters like me) that the violent reaction to the verdict was partly a result of a society in which many children grow up in communities with "more guns than grown-ups."

Rodney King and those who reacted violently to his abuse were targets of the habitual response of people in power. But let's consider another possibility.

Jesus was born into a society in which the masses were alienated. Only a few had any real status and stake in it. The great majority of the people were poor, living under the brutal authority of Roman occupation forces and unable to keep the law of God in which the devout found hope. They were subject to all sorts of mental and physical and spiritual ailments born of frustration and poverty.

Others, like the tax collectors and prostitutes, had surrendered their self-respect and were surviving by giving the Romans what they wanted—for a price. Still others ground their teeth and plotted and waited for a revolutionary leader and an opportune time to vent their hatred of Rome in a bloody uprising. But most were, as one commentator described it, "sunk without trace" in their alienated, frustrated situation.

Jesus belonged to a small class of artisans and teachers. They were alienated but not quite as impoverished as the peasant masses. And what did he do about the most alienated poor, with their seething anger and social desolation? He identified with them.

Specifically, Jesus joined with them when they were flocking to John to be baptized in the Jordan in preparation for the great day of God's intervention in their situation. He embraced their repentance and their hope of forgiveness as his own and was baptized with the others. From there he went on to proclaim the "great day"—the good news of God's kingdom: God's nearness and forgiveness and love for them all. He gave himself especially to the most alienated and oppressed: poor women and children, the sick, the possessed, the lepers, the sold out, the crazed and the crippled.

Never once did Jesus try to use the victimized masses to build a power base or make a name for himself. He spoke the unvarnished, devastating truth to the spiritual and political powers whenever they crossed his path and threatened his work. But he never, ever tried to grasp for the sort of power that was regularly used to keep the masses down. Instead, he called on them and on all his hearers to take hope, trust God, love their enemies, pray for their tormentors, and give of themselves and their goods generously for the care of neighbors in need. He taught them to return good for evil, to pray for the fulfillment of God's will of forgiveness and sustenance and justice for all. He treated everyone from saints to psychopaths with astonishing respect—as the very children of God.

And he continued this subversive, nonviolent, compassionate program to the very end—right to the cross. He didn't panic, or let his followers resort to arms. His was the way of compassion, service, and empowerment of others, of trusting in the power of God's love—the only power that can bring healing and community among alienated humans. His way is his gift to us: our calling, our mission. The shortcuts of domination and violent suppression and revenge against those who employ such methods can only produce greater alienation and conflict. This was true then and is even more urgently true in our nuclear age. It's past time to give love—Jesus' kind of love—a chance; for the hour is late.

What the way of love would have required of leaders like the first President Bush and L.A.'s Mayor Bradley, or what exactly it requires of the present leadership of our society, I don't profess to know—though I do have lots of thoughts that I would be pleased to express to such folk. But what I do know is that our leaders certainly need our prayers and encouragement, as well as our nonviolent resistance when they resort to the time-honored ways of domination and retaliation. Also, they need our example of loving alienated neighbors as ourselves, identifying with them in their pain, respecting them, and working with them as partners in eliminating the racism and poverty and other injustices that stand in the way of their full inclusion in the opportunities of our society.

In the brutality of the beating administered to Rodney King, and in the violence that erupted in response, Jesus Christ seemed to be calling and reminding us of the pain of the frustrated, neglected folk at the bottom of our society—"the least of his brothers and sisters," with whom he is so completely identified that he can say, "Inasmuch as you care for these, you do it to me."

As I imagine it, Jesus looks at the suffering of the world's oppressed and alienated, looks at a broken, devastated Rodney King and the tragic spectacle of urban violence. Then he turns and looks me in the eye and asks, as he asked Peter beside the sea after his Resurrection: "Do you love me?"

And I answer, "You know I love you, Lord."

He looks again at those alienated souls in L.A., and turns back to me: "Do you really love me?"

"You know I love you, Lord."

Then he turns and strides away, as though he's hurrying to help those who are so much in need of his healing. But he stops and turns back." Do you love me?" he asks again.

And I say, "You know everything, Lord; you know I love you."

And he beckons, "Then come with me. These alienated neighbors of yours are not to be feared; they are to be loved and respected. And as you come to know and love them and share their pain, you will grow up and learn how to love me.

"It's getting late now. We need to get on with the work for which I called you. Come on . . . Follow me."

16

About Our Meetings with Jesus

John 3:1–16

As I understand it, this story of Nicodemus' nighttime visit with Jesus is not so much about Nicodemus' meeting with Jesus as it is about anyone's meeting with Jesus. By the time John wrote his Gospel in the closing years of the first century, Nicodemus, who had been a prominent member of the Jewish power structure, was history. But he was evidently remembered by John's congregation as one who had been impressed by Jesus, and who had had a life-changing meeting with Jesus one night. So John fashioned a story based on that memory—a story intended to instruct the members of John's congregation who needed to be reminded, as we need to be reminded, of the issues at stake in our meetings with Jesus.

John tells us that Nicodemus (from here on I'll call him Nick—those three extra syllables every time he's mentioned get my tongue twisted) was a Pharisee, a ruler of the Jews. The Pharisees were the most devout and respected of the Jewish religious parties of Jesus' day—the party that survived centuries of tragic struggle to become the founders of modern Judaism. In telling this story of one of these respected Jewish leaders, John surely wanted his readers to make the connection between such a person and the influential leaders in their own Christian congregations. So when Nick speaks in this story, think of him as representing a respected member of your church: the pastor, or an elder, or at the very least a church member who is clearly drawn to Jesus—a sincere believer.

It's serious believers who have influence in the community who are being pointedly addressed by this story, and yet John also wanted his readers to see themselves in it. There's plenty in the story for skeptics who

100

are not all that impressed with Jesus. So friends, whoever you are, I invite you to open your heart and mind to Nick's story, and where the shoe fits, by all means wear it.

As the story begins, it is clear that Nick has been impressed by what he has heard about Jesus, this carpenter-turned-prophet-and-teacher from Galilee. Galilee was the "wrong side of the tracks" in the eyes of loyal Jews like the Pharisees. They called it Galilee of the Gentiles, because so many non-Jewish folk lived there. Consequently, much of what Nick had heard about Jesus before their meeting would have been negative, because Jesus was already under suspicion by the influential folk who would have made up the circle of Nick's friends. But Nick evidently thought for himself, and so he went to see what there was about Jesus that caused the poor and the afflicted to flock to him for help.

He went to see Jesus "by night." ("Nick by Night" is what one of my clever clergy friends calls this story.) Why after dark? Probably because, like most people in positions of power, Nick was unwilling to be seen as a friend of anyone as controversial as this radical character—unwilling, at least, until he had had an opportunity to talk with him face to face. I suspect that I too would have been a little cautious, a little afraid, under the circumstances.

At this first meeting with Jesus, Nick was cautious. "Rabbi," he said, " we know that you are a teacher come from God; for no one can do these signs that you do, unless God is with him." Notice that it was the "signs" of God's power at work in Jesus that had impressed him, the same way signs impress many folks today: like a power for healing, or the courage to stand up against evil practices, as Jesus did.

Such outward signs of God's power are impressive, and they draw seekers to the figures through whom they happen, whether they be Jesus, or Francis of Assisi, or Oral Roberts. So it was with Nick. Apparently. Jesus' power for good among the people had impressed him, drawn him, caused him to want to talk with Jesus about it—to test this man's ideas and convictions, and learn from him. Clearly it was a kind of faith that drew him to Jesus: a germ of faith, a fascination that I suspect most Christians share. Yet it was also a faith—like ours and that of John's readers—that was far from complete.

And so Jesus meets Nick's embryonic faith with the disturbing declaration, "Truly, I say to you, unless one is born anew, one cannot see the kingdom of God." That's a tough response, to say the least. Nick had come for discussion, hoping to have his positive feelings about this impressive teacher and healer confirmed. But Jesus, instead of thanking this admirer for his support and moving quickly to enlist him as a significant convert to his cause, confronts him with the news that unless he is born anew he shall never see the kingdom of God!

Why would Jesus talk to a prominent leader and potential disciple this way? Nick, remember, was an esteemed representative of Israel's great religious heritage—not only a Pharisee but a ruler of the Pharisees—and he had everything to lose by befriending this renegade Galilean teacher whom growing numbers of Nick's powerful friends and colleagues feared and openly held in contempt. Not only was his reputation among his peers jeopardized in this visit, but Nick's own identity—his ideas about life and the understanding of the faith of Israel that had shaped his life and given it stability—were clearly at risk in his coming to see Jesus.

Jesus knew this. So he refused to beat around the bush. "You've got to be born anew," he said. Meaning: "You've got to start all over and live a whole new kind of life, my esteemed brother. Or you'll never be able to see what I'm about and what God is up to in my ministry."

John is telling his readers in effect, "This is the way Jesus comes at folks who seem to have all the right credentials, and who enjoy the respect of the congregation. So all you saints pay attention to what Jesus is saying here. He is not impressed with your records, or your position, or with mine. His message to all of us is, you need to be born anew—need no less than a complete overhaul of your life—or you'll miss out on the joy and power and healing of this 'kingdom of God' that you've been hearing and talking and singing and preaching and praying about for so long."

Like Nick, we too have been attracted by Jesus, think well of him, have a kind of faith in him. That's why we're believers. So can he really be serious when he says we need to be reborn? That's a right heavy requirement—one that we Presbyterians, and many other mainline Christians, are generally reluctant to talk about.

No wonder Nick resisted the whole idea. "How can anyone be born after having grown old? It's impossible," he says. And it's not hard to see why. We may not have Nick's status or power or reputation but we do have whatever we have and we are what we are—and it seems more than a little drastic to require us to lay all that on the altar at this late date and start over like newborns.

Like Nicodemus, I would prefer for my life simply to be affirmed, strengthened, and blessed by my meetings with Jesus. But that's not what Jesus is about, friends. So he has to offend me, shake me out of my trust in my personal history and accomplishments, and insist that I must be born again from above: my whole life renewed and transformed by the power of God's love.

But there's something else here that causes us, as it caused Nick, to resist this demand for a complete makeover. Nick's resistance is hiding behind his question. I'm talking about the problem of our loss of hope that we really can change when we are "old." After a certain number of attempts to change the way we are, many of us—maybe all of us on occasion—cease to believe that we can change much from here on out.

Those are the times when our bright dreams of a transformed life and a better world are overcast by the clouds of past failures, and we begin to fear that it's too late for us. What we have built deed by deed and thought by thought and decision by decision is who we are—indelibly, it seems. "How can anyone be born after having grown old?" Nick's despairing question hangs over our lives like a dark cloud.

But Jesus can handle it. "Don't marvel at my saying 'You must be born anew,'" says our Lord. "The wind blows where it wills and you hear the sound of it . . ." In other words, the wind is certainly real, but it's also mysterious; and we know it only by its effects: the flags stand straight out from their flagpoles, shingles blow off houses, life as usual is suddenly disrupted. Says Jesus, "You don't know where the wind comes from or where it's going. And it's the same with everyone born of the Spirit"—everyone who is truly being born anew.

Isn't that the truth? People whose lives are being taken captive by the Spirit of Jesus are forever surprising us. They seem to be coming from some mysterious somewhere that you can't quite pin down. Things they do—the outrageously generous and compassionate and courageous things they do—cause friends and detractors alike to complain, "I don't know where she's coming from."

Some do beautiful things, like Mother Teresa; but they can also do disturbing things. They often seem too generous for their own good. They may share all they have with the poor, like my friends Murphy Davis and Ed Loring, founders of the Open Door Community, who live and work among the homeless and other rejected folk of Atlanta. They are regularly a "stench in the nostrils" of members of the city establishment, most of whom want the poor off the streets and out of sight. Theirs is an amazing story.

Those being reborn by the power of the Spirit are forever taking up with strange people, espousing unpopular causes, breaking the established society's rules—from the top. You can break the rules from the bottom, the way most of us violate the speed limits when we are in a hurry; or you can break the rules from the top, for the sake of justice and compassion and life and healing—the way Jesus did. People being born of the Spirit stick their necks out, like Jesus. You never know exactly where they're coming from or what they will do next. They are free, like the wind—like the creative Spirit of God.

That's what Jesus called Nick to be. And that's what he calls you and me to be. Jesus calls us to be "born of the Spirit"—open to the powerful leading of the Spirit of God. To be *free*, as he was free.

In saying "You must be born from above," Jesus is inviting us, as he invited old Nicodemus, to receive the gift of being ruled not by the opinions and expectations of our business associates, or our fellow church members, or even by our intimate loved ones. He's inviting us to break free from being driven and determined by the requirements of a career, or by ambition, or by the terrible addiction of accumulating and protecting and frantically consuming more stuff. He's calling us to break free from being driven and determined by the way things have "always" been done in our church, or in our community, or by "our kind of people."

Those who are born of the Spirit and led by the Spirit are free to express the love of Christ in every kind of circumstance—toward friends, toward enemies, toward all the wretched, troubled, victimized individuals and groups that others are putting down. That's the sort of personal transformation and public witness that this "born again" business is really about. It's about having our lives thoroughly changed and empowered by the Spirit of Jesus, who makes them a whole new thing.

John wrote this story as he did in order to show us that this is what meeting Jesus is really about. This being born all over again is not a matter of confirming our religious respectability or our church's great heritage. Nick was respectable aplenty, and a leader among those who were conserving his priceless Jewish heritage. But what he needed—needed terribly—and what we and our churches and our society desperately need, is to be born anew—from above—empowered by the Spirit of God to lead a whole new life of compassion and generosity and courage. A life that nothing in the institutions and privileges and technological marvels of our cyber age could ever produce. This is the gift from God that Jesus offers.

Being "born again" and "born anew" is a process, not a single event that happens once for all—say, at a Billy Graham crusade or a meeting by the lake on a spiritual retreat. The process of rebirth can get under way through the sort of religious experience that often happens in such settings. Or, alternatively, in a moment of contemplation, or of illness, or grief, or pain when we cry out to God, who draws us to Jesus for healing the way Jesus drew Nick that night.

But "born anew" is a process, consisting of many episodes and much struggle. Any moment can be an important moment in that process—so pay attention to what you may be hearing from the Spirit now. And act accordingly. Accept the freedom of the Spirit with courage and renewed hope. And be grateful that the future is as bright with promise, and grace, and beautiful surprises as it was the day you were smacked on the bottom and uttered your first statement to the world.

I seem to remember my mother telling me that she was in labor with me for sixteen hours before I was born. God has been in labor with me more than eighty years now—and still has more hard work to do in order to make good on Jesus' promise of rebirth for this old Pharisee! Thanks be to God for such endless patience, such unconquerable love. And thanks be to God for this opportunity to share with you the good news that this old story has to tell us about our meetings with Jesus.

17

Surprised?

Matthew 25:31–46

L IKE THIS SERMON, THIS story of Jesus might well be entitled "Surprise!"
Why? Because when the King and Judge of all the world says to the
righteous, "I was hungry and you fed me, thirsty and you gave me drink"
and so on, these good people are surprised.

"Lord, when did we see *you* hungry and feed you, or thirsty and give
you a drink?" they ask skeptically. Jesus answers with words that are even
more astonishing than his initial declaration: "Inasmuch as you did it to
one of the *least* of these . . . you did it to me." So intent were the righteous
on the needs of those they helped that, in caring for these neglected sufferers, the thought that they were serving the Judge of all the nations had
apparently never entered their heads. This news that they were serving
him surprises them completely!

But they are not the only ones surprised here. The wicked, too, are
very much stunned by Jesus' words. When told that they had failed to care
for the King in his hunger and thirst and loneliness and shame, they are
astonished! They can't believe they were so stupid.

So they protest: "Lord, when did we see *you* hungry, or thirsty, or a
stranger, or sick, or in prison, and not minister to you?" They are obviously thinking, "If we had only known it was you, Lord, we would have
been more than glad to help." In other words, they would have been eager
to help if they had known it would serve their self-interest—especially
their eternal self-interest!

But they were so absorbed in their own immediate needs and desires
that it had not occurred to them to care for the neglected sufferers with
whom the Judge of all the world was so completely identified. So the hor-

rendous surprise for them is the Judge's revelation, "Inasmuch as you did *not* do it to the least of these, my brothers and sisters, you did not do it to me . . . Depart from me into the eternal fire prepared for the devil and his angels." So you see, this *is* a story of surprises: a happy surprise for the righteous, a tragic surprise for the wicked.

When I started thinking about this story more carefully, it occurred to me (or maybe the Spirit said to me) that if the last Judgment turns out the way the story pictures it, you and I will have no reason to be surprised. Why? Because we know this story. Of course folks who had never heard the story could well be surprised—like those in the story. But not you and me. Most of us have heard this story repeatedly since we were little children. So none of us should be surprised when things turn out exactly this way.

These are the thoughts that brought me to the conclusion that the surprise part of the story is not the point of it—at least, not for us. Those of us who know the gospel know that Jesus is forever on the side of the hungry and poor and prisoners and outcasts of this world. We know very well that Jesus devoted his ministry to the poor, the suffering, and the excluded. That's what got him into trouble with the powerful and cost him his life. This is no surprise to us.

This realization led me to a second, more disturbing thought. Your love and my love for the hurting and the outcasts and strangers and criminals of this world can't be the sort of spontaneous unselfconscious love expressed by the "righteous" people in Jesus' story. It can't be that because we know the secret of his identification with "the least." And yet that's the kind of love that seems to be "blessed"—eternally—according to this story. So I have to ask, "Lord, is the beautiful, self-forgetful love pictured in this story the only kind of love that counts eternally?

"What about the kind of love that we promise one another in marriage—love and loyalty for better or worse, richer or poorer, in sickness and in health, whether we feel like loving or not, whether our hearts are empty or full—love that hangs in there in all the circumstances of life? Or what about the kind of love that we honor and hope for from citizens of our nation—love that cares enough to vote, to stand up and speak up for justice and compassion in our national life, a love willing to go to jail, or die, for the sake of liberty and justice for us all? Or what about the kind of parental love that we hold dear—love that understands and seeks the good of children and continues to care and work for their good even when the children are at their childish worst?

"Lord, what about your own love that caused you to land hard on religious folk who were hypocritically using their positions of privilege and leadership for their own enrichment and self-aggrandizement? Or what about the love of God as depicted elsewhere in the Bible—a love that again and again erupts in passionate outrage and judgment for the sake of a people who are destroying one another in the market place, while pretending to be devout in their worship places? Wasn't it out of love that God said, 'I hate, I despise your festivals, and I take no delight in your solemn assemblies . . . Take away from me the noise of your songs; I will not listen to the melody of your harps. But let justice roll down like waters, and righteousness like an overflowing stream' (Amos 5:21–24).

"What about these kinds of unsentimental, no-nonsense love, Lord? Aren't they real and eternally valuable?" The answer to all these questions is yes. These kinds of tough, unrelenting love are eternally valuable— every bit as valuable as the beautiful, spontaneous love that is a joy to the one who loves.

So the point of the story can't be simply that we should imitate the compassionate behavior of the goodhearted folk in the story who didn't have a clue that they were dealing with the Judge of all the world. They didn't know what they were doing, and did the right thing out of the goodness of faithful hearts, praise God. But Jesus tells the story so that we may know what they didn't know.

The message of the story is that we who are in on Jesus' secret are to be a world-transforming people who are committed to love others whether it feels good or not—no matter if all the world is hating them and excluding and damning them; no matter if our friends and neighbors and the powers that be deride us or threaten us for caring for such folk; no matter if everyone joins in the chorus, accusing us of being subversives, or communists, or "bleeding hearts."

We are to be a people committed to the welfare, dignity and salvation of those who are despised and rejected by others—no matter how marginal or lost or degraded they may be. Why? Because Jesus, the Judge of all, is forever identified with these "least sisters and brothers" of his, whom the world discounts and despises.

So who are these "least"? Poor parents who can't afford gifts for their children at Christmas? Families approved by social organizations as "needy" and worthy of food baskets at Thanksgiving? An elderly widow who needs a ride to the hospital? Well, I'm sure Jesus would have his followers care for such "deserving" poor.

But a family or an individual considered "worthy" in the eyes of the world is not what Jesus has in mind here. The "least"—the sick, the naked, the "aliens," and the prisoners in this story—are genuine social outcasts. They are people that society would have branded as unworthy.

In Jesus' world, sickness implied sin and contagion. Nakedness connoted guilt and disgrace. The same was true with the outsiders and convicts mentioned here. These people were hungry and thirsty because they were people beyond the pale, unable or unwilling to live by the accepted standards of their society and therefore rejected and excluded. The risk and probable outcome of serving such people would naturally be, as Isaiah put it and as was the case with Jesus, to be "despised and rejected" (Isaiah 53:3).

With this beautiful story, Jesus is attempting to lift us out of our natural fears of involvement with the most marginal ones among us, calling us to share the shame of those whom society casts out and hides and imprisons. He is helping us see these "least" in a completely new light—no longer as dangerous misfits, or objects of pity and charity, or threats to our personal or national security, but as sisters and brothers whom the Judge of all the world has so fully embraced in his love that he can say to us, "Inasmuch as you reach out to them, respect them, care for them, seek to understand and to serve them, *you do it to me.*"

This is the risky, dangerous kind of committed love that caused Henry Atkins, then campus minister at the University of North Carolina-Greensboro, to visit Nelson Johnson in November 1979. Nelson had been unjustly accused of inciting violence and jailed after the Greensboro Massacre, in which members of the Ku Klux Klan and American Nazi Party had opened fire on demonstrators, wounding Nelson and killing five of his fellow labor organizers. That was a time when I, along with most of Greensboro, was "asleep at the switch," paying almost no attention to what was happening to Nelson and the widows and loved ones of the five who had been murdered here. May God forgive me. May God forgive us all.

It was this same kind of dangerous, committed love that motivated those five who died that day thirty years ago. Marxists, they were—but Marxists touched by the love of God described in Jesus' Judgment scene. They gave their lives in the struggle for the rights and livelihoods and dignity of textile workers and their families.

Such dangerous, committed love can never be satisfied with pious words and praises to God and kind feelings toward abstractions like "the poor" or "humanity." The test of this kind of love occurs when the plight of the troubled stranger of the "wrong" political stripe, "wrong" educational and family background, "wrong" race, "wrong" religion, "wrong" sexual orientation claims our attention—a human being who stands there, in the flesh, in need. It is that troubled and often troublesome stranger who is to be welcomed and served as one would serve the Savior and Judge of all the world. It is in such troubled strangers—"the least"—that Jesus our Lord chooses to be present to us "all the days"(Matthew 28:20).

This is good news, not only for others, but also for us. Because the same Savior who calls to us out of our brother's or sister's need also calls to that brother or sister out of our need. As others reach out to us in our weakness and want and loneliness, they are Christ's servants to us— "christs" to us. And we may thank God, praise God, for them.

That's the way it works. Jesus has only one purpose in being identified with every least one of us. And that purpose is not to judge, but to save. His goal is to turn the heart of each of us to every other, and to bind us in one great family of justice and peace and compassion in all the earth—one beloved community. The end of all creation, I do believe, is to be a feast of love and communion from which no one is excluded—nor any included against their will.

With fear and trembling, I want to suggest an addendum to this story of the last Judgment. The way I picture it, after the Judgment scene and the welcoming of the righteous to their heavenly inheritance, Jesus rises from his seat and says to them, "Beloved, I would enjoy staying with you here. But I just can't do it. You see, those shocked souls that I just sent away from here are in terrible distress, and I can't just sit here and leave them down there to stew in the mess they've made for themselves. I must go with them and keep working with them—somehow find a way to free them from the prisons that they have built around themselves.

"I know you will understand, because I know your hearts. In fact, I suspect there are some of you who would like to come along. If so, I want you to know that you are welcome. I would be honored to have your company and your help."

And after he said that, the King and Judge of all the world descended into Hell—again. But this time he wasn't alone. A great multitude of the saints went with him, because they finally understood who he was and what he was about.

And Hell was never the same after that.

18

Does It Still Make Sense?

John 1:1–14

A s I listened to the radio recently on the way to visit friends in the hospital, the Christmas music moved without pause from "The Little Drummer Boy" to a ditty about a little girl and all her toys at Christmas. Suddenly it occurred to me how fully we have sentimentalized the birth of Jesus and how easy it is for the larger meaning of Jesus' appearance in the world to escape us.

In the midst of all the customary celebration, should we not in all honesty ask ourselves, does all of this make any sense, really? Can we honestly attach our hopes for this present world, so full of pain and sorrow, to this baby born in poverty so long ago?

After all, Jesus never became the "Christ"—a king in the proper sense—at all. True to the stories of his humble beginning, he grew up to be neither king nor priest, but a working man: a carpenter, sometime prophetic teacher and healer, who came to a bad end. Judging from the records we have, he was hardly noticed by the prominent people of his time. "Isn't this the carpenter?" asked his hometown folks in disbelief, when he taught in their synagogue early in his ministry.

Even Jesus' own family doubted the wisdom of his behavior—doubted to the point of believing he was out of his mind. And if ordinary people doubted Jesus' sanity and authority in a time when life was relatively simple and the complicated social and scientific and political complexities of our time would have been unimaginable, how then can we take him seriously as the Messiah, the revelation of God with us—in the flesh—for the sake of the world's salvation?

Let's admit it: there are real problems of belief which inevitably occur to us and our contemporaries, regardless of how our hearts are warmed by the stories of the baby and the angels and this friend of the poor and outcast who went about doing good and healing all who were oppressed by the evils of his day. To begin with, there has been since that first Christmas an incalculable change in our understanding of the physical universe. For the people of Jesus' time, the earth was at the center, heaven and its angelic hosts above, and the underworld beneath. It was hard enough for sophisticated Greeks and Romans of the ancient world to believe that what happened in a stable in Bethlehem, or years later on a hill outside Jerusalem, could have significance for the whole of their Mediterranean world.

But for us modern travelers on spaceship earth, which we know to be the merest speck whirling in a sea of limitless blackness where, for all we know, there may be an astronomical number of such specks virtually identical to ours and capable of supporting life as we know it? Surely belief in the Christmas miracle is considerably harder for moderns!

So . . . does it still make sense? Can we Christians continue to affirm blandly that the birth of this Near Eastern baby, the life and death of this Jewish carpenter-prophet whom his followers claimed was raised from the dead, is still (in addition to being a lovely memory capable of inducing warm feelings and super sales records at Christmas) the central fact of human history?

Not only our view of the universe but our moral and religious situation has changed greatly since that first Christmas, and since those days when Jesus came into Galilee preaching that the kingdom of God was at hand. It was one thing for his little band of followers—those who had experienced the power of his resurrection and expected the end of the world at any minute—to believe that Jesus Christ had conquered sin and death and all the powers of darkness once for all time. It is quite another thing for us to believe such a claim today, after twenty centuries of murderous wars and rape and exploitation and human suffering—much of it perpetrated by Christians under the banner of Jesus Christ.

Would it not be more honest simply to affirm that we do revere Jesus as a supreme moral teacher whose challenging teaching, alas, the world has been unable to embrace and put in practice—and let it go at that? Many think so these days, as we are increasingly thrown into close contact with cultured, sophisticated people of other faiths, people whose patterns of life are at many points morally superior to our own; people who are dismayed at our materialistic, lightly baptized Christianity and think us shockingly faithless and irreligious.

So my question is, in view of our present situation, with Rudolph the Red-nosed Reindeer rivaling the Angel Gabriel, and with the earth itself viewed as only a speck in an expanding universe, and with the struggle between darkness and light unabated twenty centuries after Jesus' birth, can we honestly believe that a Jewish baby of the first century really embodied the answer to humankind's religious longings? Does the message of Christmas still make sense? This question, my friends, is a question you and I must answer for ourselves. A question, mind you, that has no simple, sentimental answer.

So think with me now about the astonishing answer to our question that is recorded in the prologue to the Gospel of John, found in the first chapter. Here are some key portions of that prologue:

> *In the beginning was the Word, and the Word was with God, and the Word was God. He was in the beginning with God. All things came into being through him, and without him not one thing came into being. What has come into being in him was life, and the life was the light of all people. The light shines in the darkness, and the darkness did not overcome it . . .*
>
> *He was in the world, and the world came into being through him; yet the world did not know him. He came to what was his own, and his own people did not accept him. But to all who received him, who believed in his name, he gave power to become children of God, who were born, not of blood or of the will of the flesh or of the will of man, but of God. And the Word became flesh and lived among us, and we have seen his glory, the glory as of a father's only son, full of grace and truth.*

I think you will agree: that's not easy reading. Every word, every phrase is loaded. But the main thought, the drive of the passage, is by no means incomprehensible if we will work at understanding it. To begin with, I think we can assume that the author's intention here was surely not to confuse but to clarify. He had a vital message for the world of his time (for Jews and Gentiles alike), which he believed to be of final significance.

Also, it is reasonable to believe that those for whom John wrote this Gospel were, at the time when he wrote it, inclined to think as long and hard about the meaning of life. In fact they may have been as inclined to think about the meaning of life as we are inclined to think about the production and accumulation of things. So legends about gods and goddesses abounded in those days. Yet the divine remained, even among those who gave it thought, the Great Unknown, shrouded in mystery.

This was true even among the Jews, who believed that God had been revealed to Israel through the medium of the Word—that is, through the communication of God's will through the words of witnesses whose testimony appeared in their Scriptures. The Israelites had not seen God; yet God had (they believed) spoken covenant promises to their ancestors through servants of the divine Word. And God had kept those promises.

God had triumphed over Pharaoh in their behalf, delivered them from slavery, given them victory over their enemies, and brought them to the land of promise. God had not only kept covenant with their ancestors but had delivered the "Ten Words"—the commandments that were the heart of God's law—to Moses amid thunderings and lightnings at Sinai. And the living God had continued to speak words of judgment and grace through later servants of the divine Word: the prophets. Yahweh, their God, they had not seen; yet through God's Word spoken through Moses and the prophets, they believed they had known and encountered God.

So it was that for ancient Jews a word—whether God's or a prophet's—was not merely a sound or a symbol but the living expression of the will, the purpose, the heart and mind and spirit of the one who spoke it. It was a power that went forth from the speaker and accomplished things; a power like the opening words of Genesis when God said, "Let there be light"—and *there was light*! Or, when God said to Pharaoh, "Let my people go"—and Pharaoh was finally forced to let them go.

Consequently, when the Jews of John's day read, "In the beginning was the Word, and the Word was with God, and the Word was God," they would have been aware immediately that John was testifying concerning the very heart of their experience of God. The Word was the message of God through which God made the divine will powerfully known. For them, God's Word signified no less than the wisdom and the creative power that brought order out of chaos, that created the world and made sense of it, and gave purpose and meaning to life.

But then, not all of John's readers would have been Jews. Nevertheless this term, *word* (in Greek, *logos*), had profound meaning also for thoughtful Gentiles of the Greek-speaking culture of that time. Almost six centuries before Jesus' birth, as the Greek philosophers struggled to understand the heart of things, they too made use of the idea of the *logos* of God. They recognized that the universe was no haphazard affair; it clearly worked according to an intrinsic pattern. And though they believed the divine was invisible and beyond their reach, the basic order and reasonableness of the natural world seemed to be the expression of a divine intelligence.

So the teaching arose that God had infused all things with the divine *logos*. This *logos* was the power that caused the stars to keep to their courses, caused day and night to return in unalterable sequence. It was believed, further, that the most "divine" of human capacities—the power of reason and memory and conscience and hunger for God—were the highest work of this pervasive *logos*, or word of God. So for all of John's thoughtful readers, Jews or Greeks, the term *logos*, which we translate *word*, would have represented God, present and mysteriously at work in the universe, the basis of its order and meaning: the divine intelligence and energy whereby the world was ordered and is sustained.

When John affirmed that from "the beginning" this Word of God existed, surely the thoughtful among his readers, Christian or not, would likely have agreed. When he went on to affirm the divinity and the light and life-giving power of this Word of God, his readers, whether of Jewish or Gentile background, would likely have understood this as a reference to their world's best and highest thoughts about the mystery of God. When he then proceeded to say that this Word, this true light of God that enlightens every human being was "coming into the world"—indeed had come and been rejected "by his own people"—they would likely have begun to raise their eyebrows in puzzlement. But when they came to the incredible affirmation, "the Word became flesh"—flesh!—that weak, fragile, corruptible, mortal vehicle of and embarrassment to human existence—most would have been startled.

What?? The divine reality which fills and orders the universe, now concentrated in a weak, mortal human life? The divine becoming one of us?? For John's readers this proposition would probably have been hard to accept (as it still is today). After all, life in that world was, for most, hard—at least as hard as it is for most folks in the world in our day. It was in many ways a day-to-day struggle for survival. And God was not thought to be a part of that struggle. "That was the privilege, and the prerogative, and the advantage that a god possessed."[1]

So look at what John is doing: he has taken a concept which summed up all the highest that his readers had thought or been taught about God and uses it to introduce his story of Jesus, the carpenter from Nazareth—prophet, itinerant teacher; healer, loyal friend of the outcast: the crucified and risen Savior of the world. John's astonishing testimony to his readers, after a lifetime of experience with Jesus, both in the flesh and as his risen Lord, comes to something like this:

Everything that makes sense in our world, everything of beauty and order and meaning, was embodied in the life of this brother of us all. He is no less than "God in the flesh." If you would understand the mysteries of the created universe; if you would know the secret of the light that somehow shines in the hearts of the most hopeless of people; if you would understand the hunger for God that is in your own heart, summoning you to a better life—then you must reckon with this Jesus of Nazareth, whose story I am about to tell you.

In this Jesus, bone of our bone and flesh of our flesh, God, the Creator of all, stands revealed as fully a part of our struggle, with us in our fear and shame and pain; with us in our struggle for light amidst the world's darkness; with us and empowering us to become the very children of God, reborn by the power of God embodied in this Jesus, the only Son of the divine Father, full of grace and truth. Having seen him we have seen and experienced the very power and glory of God.

Does this message—this Word—from God still make sense? Like those ancient people for whom John wrote, many of us moderns see evidence of a divine intelligence in the workings of the universe. Also like them, many today feel alone, seeing only fleeting evidences of that intelligence in the midst of much sorrow, confusion, and darkness. Indeed, today the mystery behind it all seems even greater, and for many, even farther removed—beyond the edges of an expanding universe.

In spite of our belief that "there is a God," it is not easy to see the relation between the intelligence behind the universe, the power that makes thought possible and makes research rewarding and moral, and the story of the baby of Bethlehem, and later, the man on the cross. Can it be true that the meaning of Christmas is not exhausted by lovely stories of the baby in the manger or by our warm feelings and happy memories of the season?

What John did was set Jesus' birth in the much larger context of the eternal Word of God: the power, the intelligence, the mind of God who created all things, makes sense of all things, holds all things together in a divine love that appeared among us as Jesus, fully human. Jesus, who shared our struggle, even to death, as the only Son of a loving Father whose grace fills all things and can empower you and me to become the children of God that God always intended us to be. That's what Christmas is about, according to John. And, friends, as astonishing as it sounds, to me it still makes sense.

ENDNOTES

1. Gossip, *The Interpreter's Bible*, Vol. 8, 473.

19

God Frees Us for Beloved Community

Exodus 3:1–12

A UTHOR'S NOTE: *JESUS' DECLARATION of the good news that the king-dom of God was "at hand" in his ministry was nothing less than an announcement of the fulfillment of his people's hopes. As Jesus proceeded to bring his healing, liberating news to the broken and marginalized masses among the Jews, their established leaders found his message threatening— so threatening in fact that they conspired with the Romans to have him crucified.*

But death was no match for the saving purpose of God that Jesus embodied.

Jesus had shown the society of his day that Israel's gracious God sought the liberation of all humanity to share in the joy and peace of beloved community as the children of God. His resurrection was in truth the liberation of Jesus' spirit to continue his work through his followers, whom he continues to call still today into his ministry of liberation.

Sad to say, we who follow Jesus often suffer un-liberated moments when we picture and preach Jesus in terms that set him over against the God to which the Old Testament bears witness. Such moments divide Christians from our Jewish brothers and sisters whose religious roots we share. So I in-clude the following reflection on the God of the Bible as the eternal Liberator of us all at the end of this collection of sermons on the Gospels, to help readers avoid the perennial temptation to see the "Old Testament God" as somehow different from and inferior to the God and Father of Jesus celebrated in these pages. And as a concluding summary of the heart of the message.

I preached this sermon to a very mixed congregation—Christian and Jewish, black and white, believers and nonbelievers—at Faith Community Church in Greensboro, North Carolina, on September 20, 2009.

Picture yourself in Pharaoh's place. Moses, rescued from genocide as a Hebrew baby and reared as a prince in your royal court—and now a known murderer who has fled the country—suddenly reappears on the palace doorstep with a ridiculous demand from a god you never heard of. "Let my people go!" is this god's blunt demand. The people in this case are slave laborers whom you are using to build new cities for storing the plunder of your empire.

So how would you answer such a demand if you were Pharaoh? Imagine that you are the proud ruler of the number-one nation of the world and a god in the eyes of your own people—confronted by this rabble-rousing labor organizer, Moses, and told to release your workers so that they can go out into the desert and worship their rabble-rousing god. Would you let them go? I venture to doubt it; that's just not the way the powers of this world work.

It would be like having some Harvard-educated labor-organizer-turned-preacher claim he has a mandate from God to push the president of the United States into disrupting the economy and threatening the nation's food supply—all for the sake of some migrant farm workers. Disadvantaged and exploited minorities have always been present in powerful nations, unfortunately. But should the needs of such people determine public policy? Should ordinary, law-abiding citizens suffer inconvenience or loss on their account?

"I will not let them go!" said Pharaoh, speaking from the perspective of the powers of this world. Instead, he proceeded to make their work harder, requiring them to "make their bricks without straw" (see Exodus 5:7–9). Pharaoh's response to Moses and company was typical of the responses of the powerful to the pleas and demands of the troublesome Moses types who from time to time rattle society's chains.

This NO! of the powerful may be accompanied by brutal repression. Or lacking the stomach for that, the powerful may conspire with thugs who are willing to do their dirty work for them, as some of our Greensboro authorities conspired with the Ku Klux Klan and Nazis in 1979 to bring about the massacre of five labor organizers working with laborers in the textile mills. The response of the powerful to the powerless has been essentially the same through the centuries: "Sit down and shut up, *or else!*" Such is the spirit of those who are determined to dominate others.

But the strange God who got Moses' attention and sent him to tell Pharaoh "Let my people go!" speaks in a very different spirit. This God—this liberating God of Israel—had said to Moses: "I have seen the affliction of my people . . . and have heard their cry because of their taskmasters; I know their sufferings, and I have come . . . to deliver them from the Egyptians. So come, I will send you to Pharaoh that you may bring forth my people" (Exodus 3:7–10).

With these words, the God of the Bible first appears in the full light of history as a liberator of the oppressed—and the eternal enemy of every form of slavery and oppression. This is the oldest story in the Book, the formative story for Israel's life and worship as a community (see Deuteronomy 26:5–10). This is who Israel's God was from the nation's beginning as a people, and who their "living God" would be forevermore. The God of the Bible, Creator of all, is the determined Liberator of all who are enslaved and exploited. This includes the victims of slavery in our nation's past and of continuing racism in its present. It also includes the children abroad who make our clothes and the migrants who raise the crops that nourish us.

Unfortunately, popular notions of God—along with many stories in the Bible—present God as the most powerful of all the powers that be, the heavenly King of Kings and Lord of Lords who can "out-Pharaoh" any Pharaoh. But some strands of the Bible's testimony point to Israel's deeper understanding of God as the compassionate fellow sufferer and Liberator who deeply feels the pain of all the oppressed.

A prime example is the Ten Commandments, which begin with the words, "I am the Lord your God who brought you out of the land of Egypt, out of the house of bondage" (Exodus 20:2; Deuteronomy 5:7). These commandments, the very heart of the Law of Moses, are to be understood not as the burdensome requirements of a heavenly dictator but as the indispensable basis for life as God would have it lived: in a community of free people in which all members are valued, loved, and respected. They are a succinct expression of the will of Israel's compassionate Liberator for this people's new life of faith, freedom, and mutual respect.

Time and again in the Bible, humane laws that are unparalleled in the ancient world testify to the merciful, liberating character of Israel's God by including the reminder, "You shall remember, you were a slave in the land of Egypt and the Lord your God brought you out" (Leviticus 19:33, 25:55; Deuteronomy 6:12, 8:14, 15:15, 16:12). This reminder was used in reference to laws such as the Sabbath commandment, which provided one day's rest in seven for everybody, including slaves and aliens, and even the farmers' livestock (Deuteronomy 5:12–15). Even the land itself was to be given a Sabbath rest and allowed to lie fallow—free!—every seventh year (Exodus 23:10–11; Leviticus 25:1–7).

Taking the Sabbath concept a step further, the law of Israel's Liberator God required forgiveness of debts every seventh year and release of those who had fallen into slavery because of their indebtedness. It also mandated that the slaves who were freed not be sent away empty-handed, but that they be equipped with a liberal share of the goods that they had helped to produce during their slavery (see Deuteronomy 15:1–17).

In the same spirit, God's law required prosperous farmers not to be too efficient in harvesting their crops, so that the poor might glean what was left in their fields and orchards and vineyards and not go hungry (see Leviticus 19:9–10; Deuteronomy 24:19–22). It prohibited lenders from taking interest on loans to the poor (Exodus 22:25; Leviticus 25:35–38), and it required that a poor man's garment, if taken as collateral for a loan, be returned to him at sundown, so he wouldn't suffer from the cold during the desert night (Exodus 22:26–27).

What a shocking contrast to the predatory lending practices of our day! Most generous of all was the law of the Jubilee, which required that every fiftieth year all debts were to be forgiven and *all* slaves freed. Families were to return to their ancestral inheritances, and land that had been lost through debt or misfortune was to be returned to the families to whom God had originally given it when Israel arrived in the Promised Land (see Leviticus 25).

We have no way of knowing how faithfully such provisions were carried out during Israel's history. What is clear is that the spirit that inspired those generous provisions of Israel's law was the Spirit of Israel's Liberator God, whose will for these former slaves was that they live their freedom as a community of love and equality, justice and peace. In God's name, Israel's prophets again and again called the people to honor their obligation to practice this kind of just and compassionate inclusion of the vulnerable and the oppressed and the aliens among them in the life of their communities. So it is abundantly clear that Israel's entire social and economic order was deeply affected by this people's experience of God as first of all and forever the Great Liberator.

What God intended for these freed slaves was that in their dealings with one another, especially with the disadvantaged and vulnerable among them, they should reflect the character of their God. This was their unique mission in the world. All of this stands in stark contrast to the world of competition and domination that later prevailed in Israel and in which we live today. In our world we are always tempted, and regularly encouraged, to use our personal gifts and opportunities for our own self-advancement and pleasure, at the expense of those who are disadvantaged.

In the clash of human wills and desires in our competitive society, we early learn to make the most of our assets, using what our culture values as advantages (such as being white, or being male, or being heterosexual, or being rich) to get the better of others and to advance ourselves. As a result, the less gifted (in society's eyes) inevitably suffer. So it is that the fullness of life that God intends for us all is blocked. If all are to have a chance in such a world, those with such culturally determined advantages must be liberated to use their gifts not in self-serving, dominating ways but in service and sharing with all. Otherwise there can be no peace, no community, and no hopeful future.

Our choice in this modern world seems to be community or catastrophe, life or death. We absolutely must learn what the Israelites learned the hard way after their arrival in the Promised Land. When these former slaves were finally settled in their new home, enjoying the blessings of freedom, they discovered that their God's passion for freedom and justice was a two-edged sword. In Egypt, where they were slaves, it had led to their liberation. But when they became oppressors of the poor and vulnerable among them, it led to their destruction.

This lesson was indelibly stamped on Israel's life in the course of its experience with the liberating God of the Exodus. It was God's passion for the liberation of the oppressed that called forth the prophets' terrible denunciations of the people's exploitation of their poor neighbors. The prophets gave powerful testimony to God's hatred of the pious behavior and worship that the people were enthusiastically substituting for basic social justice and care for one another. God's passion for the liberation of all was the basis of the prophets' urgent calls to repentance and their warnings of certain disaster if there was no repentance.

This is the passion that Jesus embodied in all that he said and did. As Luke tells it, Jesus embraced as his platform these words from Isaiah 61, recalling the Jubilee "year of the Lord's favor":

> *The Spirit of the Lord is upon me,*
> *because he has anointed me*
> *to bring good news to the poor.*
> *He has sent me to proclaim release to the captives*
> *and recovery of sight to the blind,*
> *to let the oppressed go free,*
> *to proclaim the year of the Lord's favor.* (Luke 4:16–21)

Rather than allying himself with the "great ones" of his society, Jesus came on the scene in the Spirit of the God who told Moses, "I have seen the affliction of my people and have heard their cry . . . I know their sufferings, and I have come to deliver them." Jesus spent most of his days not among the rich and powerful of his day but with the poor. He lived among and identified with the impoverished masses, liberating those labeled demon-possessed, sick, and unclean, restoring them to full and respected membership in the community.

In his teaching, Jesus drew on the experience of farm workers, slaves, day laborers, and beggars who were vulnerable to the uncertainties of nature and the whims of the masters and employers who dominated their lives. He couched his message in stories filled with the details of their humble village life: stories of farmers and all sorts of laborers at work; of children at play; of women going about their daily tasks in kitchen and home, living lives of courage and compassion in that male-dominated society. He captured the realities of the experience of these ordinary, mostly forgotten or unappreciated folk as windows into, and parables of, the reality of God's presence and purpose at work in the world.

By eating with the excluded and the neglected, and empowering their faith through his love and affirmation, Jesus claimed all of them as God's beloved children. Like the prophets before him, he taught rich and poor alike that the final issue of life—the measure of the life of the nations of earth on the Day of Judgment—would not be their creedal professions or their impressive worship and piety, much less their wealth or power. It would be their care for—or their neglect of—the "least" among them: the hungry, the thirsty, the stranger, the naked, the sick, and the prisoner. "Inasmuch as you did it to the least of these, my brothers and sisters, you did it to me" was to be Jesus' final verdict as the Son of the liberating God of all (Matthew 25:40).

As Jesus saw it, the final significance of our lives will depend on whether we use our gifts and goods in the healing of the human community, or for our own pleasure and profit and to curry favor with those who can return our favors. "If you do good to those who do good to you, what credit is that to you?" he asked (Luke 6:32). That is the way of the world. But to be a real friend to the troubled, the broken, and the excluded, including enemies—and to use our gifts and resources in the service of those from whom we can expect nothing in return—that is the way of the Great Liberator, the way of Jesus Christ our Lord.

Does this mean that God is opposed to the gifted and privileged? No. Jesus was gifted and privileged, but the difference between him and many others of his day was that he identified with and devoted his gifts to the service of those who were oppressed and forgotten. In the name of the liberating God, he loved the struggling masses, forgave them, embraced them in all their brokenness and incomprehension of what he was about, and invited them to the inclusive community of love that he was creating wherever he went. Yet he was present to all sorts of others too, including the powerful and privileged, the pious scribes and temple establishment and others, engaging their fears and their resistance and their criticism with unwavering courage and honesty, refusing to give up on any of them.

God's desire, as Jesus embodied it, was a community in which there were no first- and second-class members, and no expendables—a beloved and loving community in which all were equally loved by God, and all equally called to love God and to love and forgive one another as freely and generously as they themselves had been loved and forgiven. In that spirit, he was as honest and available to his self-righteous critics and adversaries as he was to the struggling masses. He minced no words about the blindness of the powerful and refused to be controlled by their self-serving piety and customs, or to be cowed. They hated and feared this astonishingly free man and made it their business to silence his subversive message by seeing to his crucifixion.

So it comes to this: God is not calling us to be heroes and heroines who on occasion forsake our comfort zones and offer handouts and used clothing and kindly smiles to those whom we deem worthy of our charity or our tax dollars or our friendship. There is nothing wrong with charitable work with the poor or with befriending people in high places, who certainly need honest, caring friends. But God is calling us to be *free*—dangerously free and passionately honest with all for the sake of their liberation and ours. God is calling us to follow in Jesus' way of identification with all who are captives in our time—all who are being corrupted and destroyed by the greedy, fearful, dark side of our prosperity and power.

This means identification with the unemployed and unemployable, with disadvantaged minorities and immigrants, with parents who slave away for less than a living wage, with the sick children of poverty, with drug addicts and the homeless and the growing multitude of prisoners locked in cages across this land. But it also means identification with those who are addicted to their own privilege and power, blinded by greed and by fear of loss of their wealth and status and power over others, which they trust for the meaning of their lives.

God wants to free us *all*. So Jesus is calling us to take off our self-serving blinders, confront our own captivity, and see the suffering people around us; to feel their pain and become involved with them in their liberation and ours, their healing and ours. Like Jesus, we are to show the world the good news of God's will for us all: a beloved human community in which there is love enough, respect enough, forgiveness enough, and food and care and dignity enough, for everyone's fulfillment as a beloved child of God.

This requires organizing and challenging and changing things, like Moses, and Jesus, and Gandhi, and Martin Luther King, and Joyce and Nelson Johnson and others around Greensboro's Beloved Community Center whose liberating spirits are touching neighbors' lives and helping them break free to pursue God's will for justice and peace. For the truth is that only in that kind of struggle for life and community can we experience our own liberation as servants of our rabble-rousing, liberating God, who will be with us all the way!

Appendix 1

The Beloved Community Center:
Statement of Commitment

BELIEVING THAT A SPIRIT of domination, alienation, and violence regularly undermines the hope of community in our society, we have committed ourselves to the embodiment and propagation of an alternative spirit of persistent good will toward all members of society in pursuing what Dr. M. L. King, Jr. called "beloved community." That is, just and compassionate social and economic relations that affirm the dignity, worth, and potential of every person.

In this spirit we share a commitment to identify with and advocate for those who are oppressed, demeaned, or marginalized by present social structures: blacks and other minority ethnic groups, the poor, women, homosexuals—all who suffer from historical, structural, personal, and other forms of discrimination and injustice. We are committed not only to advocate for and with these sisters and brothers but to engage and resist the ignorance, confusion, attitudes, customs, and powers of domination and distortion under which they suffer.

To this end, we are committed to a fundamental strategy of imaginative, nonviolent resistance and engagement in the spirit of Jesus, Gandhi, and King. We believe that hate begets hate, that violence is not the solution to social evils, and that a spirit of vengeance can never be creative of community. While we affirm our responsibility and society's responsibility to restrain by necessary means those who oppress or abuse its vulnerable and defenseless members, our final trust is in the power of truth, spoken and embodied in love, to overcome "spin" and lies and other manifestations of the spirit of domination, alienation, and war.

We confess that we ourselves are deeply infected with the tendencies to fight evil with evil, or worse, to let the seductive power of evil co-opt us in its service. Therefore we are committed to a disciplined process of inner struggle, study, and transformation within our own alternative community, as we work for transformation in society at large.

Further, we affirm that this statement of our commitments is provisional; that is, it is open to amendment as necessitated by the experiences and insights we encounter as we grow together. For example, we have only recently begun to recognize fully our need to enlarge our understanding of beloved community to embrace not only human relationships but our relations with all species—indeed, with all creation. So we will be developing this area of personal and communal growth and transformative practice in the future.

Finally, we affirm that we have come to our hope for beloved community by a variety of paths: some by way of Christian faith, others by civil rights and labor struggles, and some by other faiths and ideologies. Therefore we welcome to our quest all who share the fundamental commitments expressed here, regardless of their religious or ideological orientation. Come, help us grow, and grow with us, toward the realization of the beloved community for which, we believe, all things exist.

Author's Note: *Faith Community Church is a small, mostly African American congregation that shares the facilities and the commitments expressed in the Statement of Commitment above. It is welcoming of all the diverse individuals and groups who are a part of the BCC's work. However, its worship and its teaching are very specifically Christian in the African American tradition.*

Appendix 2

The Servant Leadership School of Greensboro: Statement of Purpose

A CORE BELIEF OF our school is that every church in the world, by nature, is called to prepare servant leaders to follow Jesus Christ and serve God's dream for a transformed world. The Servant Leadership School of Greensboro invites students to a deeper relationship with God and with others in community, as we explore both an inward journey of personal transformation and an outward journey of discerning our own particular "call" and giving expression to some form of life-giving service in the world. We have welcomed participants from a wide variety of churches and organizations. We have supported persons called to serve in ministries of compassion, justice, and the alleviation of human suffering. Additionally, we have encouraged those called to practice servant leadership in their daily life and work, bringing new life to relationships, businesses, groups, and organizations of all kinds. Our hope is to nurture a generation of Christian leadership which will bring renewal to our churches, create life-giving alternatives in the workplace, call forth creative new ministries to serve our community, and help to shape our future in accordance with God's dream.

Appendix 3

A Plea to the Christian Churches of Greensboro

*(Written in behalf of the Greensboro Truth
and Community Reconciliation Project for inclusion
in weekly church bulletins)*

We are members of the Local Task Force of the
Greensboro Truth and Community Reconciliation Project.
None of us is a member of the Greensboro Truth and
Reconciliation Commission. That is a separate entity which
was selected through an open process in which all citizens
of Greensboro were invited to participate. It is charged
with "examination of the context, causes, sequence, and
consequence" of the tragic events of November 3, 1979.
The Commission's mandate stipulates that it will carry out
its work "while operating independently from any external
influence, including the Project" which we represent.

We are well aware of suspicion in the community that
the Project, which includes survivors of the shootings of
November 3, 1979, will unfairly influence or determine the
Commission's findings. Not so. The process that brought the
Commission into being and the Mandate under which it is
carrying out its independent inquiry are intended to free it
to pursue the truth without fear or favor. Its members are
persons of unimpeachable integrity. They need and deserve
the confidence, respect, and full cooperation of all citizens

of Greensboro. In the interest of truth that can set us all free from the confusion and distrust related to the tragedy of 1979, we urge all citizens of Greensboro to give their full and enthusiastic support to the Commission as it seeks personal testimony and other relevant information that can lead to a full, deeply human and healing understanding of the events surrounding that tragedy.

Friends, we would make our case for your support for the Commission with the help of Jesus' words from the Sermon on the Mount. There he warned his hearers of the power of unresolved anger and accusations to rob us of our freedom: *Settle matters quickly with your adversary who is taking you to court. Do it while you are still with him on the way, or he may hand you over to the judge . . . and you may be thrown into prison. I tell you the truth, you will not get out until you have paid the last penny.* (Matthew 5:25–26)

With these words in mind, think back to that labor rally of November 3, 1979, where five persons were shot dead and ten others wounded. As a community we have somehow been unable to free ourselves from the rage that erupted that day. We took the killers "to court"—three different times. They were acquitted of wrongdoing. But within the community, anger and accusations persisted among those who had been terrorized by the incident. We blamed the Communist organizers of the rally, blamed the Klan-Nazi group who did the killing, blamed Greensboro's Police and officialdom for failing to prevent it, blamed the media for their reporting of it. But as a community we have not troubled ourselves to get to the full truth in and behind the confusing stories that still surround those shootings, dividing us from our neighbors and weakening trust in our public institutions.

When our Project proposed some months ago that Greensboro engage in a process of truth seeking that would enable us to resolve our confusion and facilitate reconciliation of all concerned, there was widespread reluctance to reopen this painful chapter of our history. Many felt, and feel still, that we need instead to focus on the present and future challenges to our city's social and economic well-being. And yet . . . a "social capital" study undertaken recently by our Community Foundation revealed a serious lack of "public trust" among our citizenry, which makes it difficult for us to come together in facing the challenges before us.

That study revealed that we have failed to "settle matters quickly" among the adversarial groups whose differences fueled the November 3 tragedy and the angry, accusatory confusion that has surrounded it ever since. Consequently, we are "imprisoned" by our public distrust.

It is also apparent that among those reluctant to join in this struggle for community reconciliation are many Christian people. So we ask: Should followers of Jesus pass up this unique opportunity to learn the truth that just might set us all free from our prisons of distrust? Listen to Jesus again: "If you are offering your gift at the altar, and there re-member that your brother [or sister] has something against you, leave your gift there in front of the altar. First go and be reconciled to your brother; then come and offer your gift" (Matthew 5:23–24).

Christian friends, many of us forgot something on the way to church. We forgot to be reconciled first to a crowd of folks who "have something against us": the victims and shooters and police and media, and all the others who have suffered blame or condemnation or other trauma related to November 3, 1979. Shouldn't we first go, all of us, and support the quest for truth and community reconciliation among us?—then return to our churches, free of fear and rancor, and offer God the gift of a community healed of a painful episode of its past and empowered to face its future with renewed courage and hope.

In faith, hope, and love, and on behalf of the Greensboro Truth and Community Reconciliation Project, Z Holler